Hope
in
Process

Hope
in
Process

**A Theology of
Social Pluralism**

Henry J. Young

Fortress Press   **Minneapolis**

HOPE IN PROCESS
A Theology of Social Pluralism

Scripture quotations unless otherwise noted are from the Revised Standard Version of the Bible, copyright © 1946, 1952, and 1971 by the Division of Christian Education of the National Council of Churches.

Cover photo: Ned Skubic

Cover design: Terry W. Bentley

Library of Congress Cataloging-in-Publication Data

Young, Henry J., 1943–
    Hope in process : a theology of social pluralism / Henry J. Young.
        p.   cm.
    Includes bibliographical references.
    ISBN 0-8006-2397-5
    1. Sociology, Christian—United States.   2. Pluralism (Social sciences)—United States.   3. Race relations—Religious aspects—Christianity.   4. United States—Race relations.   5. Process theology.   6. Liberation theology.   7. Black theology.   I. Title.
BR517.Y68   1989
261.8'34'0973—dc20   89-37507
                                             CIP

The paper used in this publication meets the minimum requirements of American National Standard for Information Sciences–Permanence of Paper for Printed Library Materials, ANSI Z329.48-1984   ∞™

Manufactured in the U.S.A.   AF 1-2397

94   93   92   91   90   1   2   3   4   5   6   7   8   9   10

In memory of
John A. Hollar

Contents

Foreword

Social analysts have brilliantly exposed the many-faceted oppressions from which most human beings have suffered throughout historical times. Most important, they have made us aware of how our own society perpetuates many forms of oppression and even develops new ones. This conscientization has been an immensely valuable contribution to human maturation, especially in the past quarter century.

The response of people of goodwill to new awareness of oppression is to call for liberation and justice. This is admirable, and it is only as more people join in this commitment that desirable change is likely to occur. But the problems are complex, and they cannot be solved by goodwill alone.

A case in point is the success of Martin Luther King, Jr., in leading the nation away from legalized segregation toward legalized integration. This was an immense accomplishment for which King has been rightly recognized as one of America's greatest leaders. Yet few would claim that the black-white problem has been solved. While millions of blacks have successfully integrated, the majority have not.

One reason for the failure of integration is the continuing racism of the majority community, although this is not the whole story. Another problem is that the ideal of integration assumes the acceptance of the normativeness of the dominant white culture with its built-in individualism and dualism. The price of integration is the abandonment of a more holistic black culture. The alternative seems to be racial separation. Yet separation inside a nation dominated by an alien culture is no solution either.

Henry J. Young addresses this problem, seeking a third option. This not only entails a different strategy or goal for the black community and other ethnic minority groups. It also requires a paradigm shift for the dominant culture.

Young rightly recognizes that paradigm shifts do not come easily. There cannot be a shift of models for social change apart from a shift of religious and philosophical sensibility. As long as we think of the units of reality as self-contained and mutually external, the only options will be for ethnic groups to retain their separated identity, to abandon it in assimilation to the dominant group, or to strike a compromise between these programs.

Young finds a different model in Whitehead's philosophy. Here each individual is both intimately interconnected with all the others and still unique in his or her own particularity. There is no need to choose between a diversity of mutually influencing parts. The unity of the whole is a dynamic and changing one. No one part can define what is normative for the others or for the whole, for each is influenced by all the others.

Young is not alone, of course, in calling for unity in diversity as the national goal. While he does not go far toward spelling out the social and economic forms that would embody this ideal, what he does accomplish is to make remarkably clear the sharp contrast between this model and the ones that remain dominant today. Indeed, he shows how the new model is connected to a larger paradigm shift already in process in physics, philosophy, and theology. This is no mean achievement!

The United States has gone through a decade of reaction in which the cultural normativity of one strand of its heritage has been loudly affirmed. The advocates of pluralism have been on the defensive in many areas. Until a positive image of unity in diversity can be formulated in a convincing way, we will be condemned to choosing between sheer pluralism and a homogeneous unity. Young's proposal is a vision of hope.

There is more to Young's book. In fact the book is as much a proposal for theology as a proposal for society. Young thinks holistically and sees that only as theological method becomes pluralistic can theology give real support to a healthy social pluralism.

As a process theologian I particularly appreciate chapter 4. Here Young confronts Whitehead's vision of God with the agenda of black liberation. He does so as a competent interpreter of Whitehead, appreciative of much that Whitehead has contributed. He does so also as one truly committed to the ending of black oppression. The result is a valuable critique not only for process theologians but for all who struggle to understand God with sensitivity to the realities of our world.

JOHN B. COBB, JR.

Preface

A new ethnic consciousness is sweeping over the global village. Afro-Americans, Latin Americans, Africans, Asian Americans, Hispanics, Mexican Americans, American Indians, and women in all ethnic communities are protesting the inability of more traditional approaches to overcome the sexism, racism, classism, provincialism, ethnocentricism, and imperialism of the old order's approach to pluralism. I call this a new ethnic consciousness because it seeks to reconceptualize and reorient radically the relations of majority groups to minority groups. Old, established racial stereotypes, prejudices, fears, and distortions that have oppressed minority social groups and pushed them to the margins of society are now being challenged, repudiated, and even dismantled by those groups.

My contention is that traditional approaches to social pluralism — both in America and in the global village — are grounded in the inadequacies of the modern scientific world view. Because these inadequacies inform and dominate our theory and practice, they continue to engender or sustain various forms of dualism, a monocultural ethos, a deterministic approach to human volition, a mechanical interpretation of reality, thoroughgoing individualism, an exploitation of human resources, and an instrumental view of the environment. Consequently, both the cultural insulation between social groups and the inequitable distribution of resources are perpetuated in spite of efforts to achieve a peaceful coexistence between majority and minority social groups. To achieve this state — the basis of a true cultural pluralism — it is necessary for us to find a viable alternative to the root of sexism and racism, to find a ground for our vision of reality and society that avoids the classism of the present. My thesis is that the organic pluralism espoused by Alfred North Whitehead provides a better basis for constructing a vision of social pluralism that can elide these social ills. In his thought on the reality of God, the nature of human existence, the world of nature, and the meaning of ultimate reality, Whitehead overcame the inadequacies of the modern scientific world view. In these areas, he created a revolution in metaphysical construction and fostered a shift in paradigms, from a closed, dualistic world view to an open, organic one. In this book, I draw out the implications of this shift in world view for majority-minority relations — something that philosophers of science, theologians, social scientists, and behaviorists have been hesitant to do.

That human liberation begins with shifting world views is central to my thesis. When Whitehead maintained that "the fallacy of misplaced concreteness" was at the base of the modern scientific world, he introduced such a shift to our modern consciousness. Modern humanity, he stated, treats the abstract as though it were the concrete and so distorts all acts of human experience. For modern humanity to overcome these distortions in the social realm, our whole understanding of majority-minority relations needs to be changed. Such a reorientation or liberation can be achieved only through a shift in world views.

Through my survey of America's ethnic context, it is evident that these distortions, nurtured by misplaced concreteness, have created another set that I term "the fallacy of misplaced cultural identity." By this I mean that a group's identity is fixated in a posture of closed nationalism grounded in a self-contained, narrow, and one-sided framework. That is to say, each group seeks to reduce cultural pluralism, the abstraction, to its own concreteness. This fallacy gives rise to the cultural distortions manifested as sexism, racism, classism, provincialism, ethnocentricism, and imperialism. My call for a shift in modern consciousness, then, expresses the need for an open nationalism, based on cultural relativity, one that facilitates liberating possibilities. My goal is to think through the theological implications of the Whiteheadian model of organic pluralism, and then to determine what those implications mean for cultural pluralism as related to intergroup relations.

Within a socio-historical frame, chapter 1 examines and critiques the traditional approaches to pluralism in America. The inadequacies present in the modern scientific world view have engendered social ills between majority and minority social groups. These social ills have culminated in the problem of Anglo conformity and cultural normativeness. From philosophical, theological, and social perspectives, I shall show the ways in which this problem has inhibited the formation of a model of cultural pluralism that is void of sexism, racism, and classism.

Chapter 2 draws upon Whitehead's idea of organic pluralism and shows how this can be used as the context for a radical shift in our concept of majority-minority relations. By integrating this organic pluralism into a model of cultural pluralism, I will develop the needed reconceptualization.

Chapter 3 discusses the implications of organic pluralism for reconstructing theological method. Multi-ethnic social groups and sources of theology are brought together to construct a paradigm that I believe will be useful for most if not all minority groups in their religious reflection on social realities.

Chapter 4 tests the implications of an organic, social conception of God for its liberating significance for the oppressed. There I expose the strengths and weaknesses of Whitehead's persuasive ethical theism. My conclusion is that there is "hope in process" — a hope of overcoming the majority-minority dichotomy.

Completion of this project was made possible by a sabbatical leave from Garrett-Evangelical Theological Seminary during the 1986–87 academic year. A portion of the leave was spent at the Center for Process Studies at Claremont School of Theology, Claremont, California, where I made presentations of sections of the manuscript to faculty members and students.

John B. Cobb, Jr., director of the Center for Process Studies at Claremont, Ingraham Professor of Theology at the School of Theology at Claremont, and Avery Professor in the Claremont Graduate

School, read the entire manuscript and made invaluable suggestions for revisions. For John's critical appraisal and encouragement, I will always be grateful. David Ray Griffin, professor of the philosophy of religion, Claremont School of Theology, read a portion of the manuscript and also made useful criticisms and suggestions. Gene Reeves, dean of Meadville/Lombard Theological School in Chicago, read the entire manuscript and made helpful comments. Thomas Hoyt, Jr., professor of New Testament interpretation, the Hartford Seminary Foundation, Hartford, Connecticut, reviewed a portion of the manuscript and raised vital questions concerning both methodology and content. Rosemary Radford Ruether, Georgia Harkness Professor of Applied Theology, and James E. Will, Henry Pfeiffer Professor of Systematic Theology, Garrett-Evangelical Theological Seminary, responded to an early version of chapter 2 presented at an annual faculty retreat.

An early version of chapter 4 was presented during a conference on process theology and liberation theology in November 1985 at the Divinity School, University of Chicago. The conference was cosponsored by Meadville/Lombard Theological School, Chicago Theological Seminary, the Divinity School of the University of Chicago, and Garrett-Evangelical Theological Seminary. Gene Reeves served as chairperson of the conference.

If any errors or mistakes in interpretation appear, I accept full responsibility for them.

1

The Inadequacy of Traditional Approaches to Pluralism in America

Anglo Conformity and Cultural Normativeness

What keeps social pluralism from benefiting both majority and minority social groups in America and elsewhere? The answer is Anglo conformity: the demand that minority social groups conform to the values of the white majority social group. Anglo conformity prescribes the norms for intergroup relations.

The Norm of Nativism

That this cultural normativeness has proved inadequate I take to be obvious. Equally obvious are its social implications. The history of immigrant groups in the United States demonstrates clearly the dominance of Anglo-Saxon consciousness. The Anglo-Saxon Protestant group dominated because its members were "most similar in race, culture and religion to the earliest colonists."[1] Accompanying this is the presumption that the United States is a function of the Anglo-Saxon race. Other immigrant groups became assimilated into American society only by conforming to this norm. Patriotism —

1

devotion to America — is particularly identified with this Anglo conformity.[2] To be recognized as American, other social groups have been constrained to adopt as their own the Anglo-Saxon cultural standards rather than having been encouraged to cultivate their own heritages. Social acceptance of minority social groups has been contingent upon their embracing the language, customs, values, and life-style of the "nativist" white Anglo-Saxon Protestants.[3] Because Anglo conformity functioned as a norm, social scientists developed theories to account for the eventual assimilation of minorities into the dominant culture. In time, ethnic diversity would be dissolved into a single strand of ethnic unity, or so the theories went.[4]

Both cannot be done: acknowledging that America consists of diverse ethnic social groups on the one hand, and developing ideologies, social philosophies, and theologies geared toward perpetuating cultural normativeness on the other hand. Many have resolved the contradiction by denying the diversity. For example, Oscar Handlin said in 1951, "Once I thought to write a history of the immigrants in America. Then I discovered that the immigrants were Americans."[5] For me, however, the critical issue is not to debate whether America contains diverse ethnic groups but rather is to find ways of overcoming cultural normativeness. Models of assimilation and acculturation will enable ethnic groups to realize their respective cultural identities.

The Minority Reality of Double-consciousness

The assimilation process in America, as I have said, assumes that unity means conformity to the culture of the Anglo-American majority social group. Anything to the contrary is considered unacceptable. The Anglo majority, then, tends to feel racially superior; and this cultural normativeness has led to a social crisis for Afro-Americans and other minority groups.

W. E. B. Du Bois, the pioneering authority in race relations, adopted a double-consciousness typology in order to discuss this social crisis. Double-consciousness means always to look at oneself through the eyes of others, to measure oneself by the cultural standards of the majority social group, which in this country looks at Afro-Americans with "amused contempt and pity," refusing to yield to Afro-Americans their own, true self-consciousness.[6] The social crisis is a dilemma reflected in the individual's sense of being an American *and* an Afro-American; there is a "twoness": two levels of consciousness, two perspectives, and two seemingly unreconciled realities, "two warring ideas in one dark body, whose dogged strength alone keeps it from being torn asunder."[7]

The history of the Afro-American experience is the manifestation of this struggle; it is a search to attain authentic self-consciousness, to bring to this double-consciousness an expression of genuine cultural pluralism without losing a profound sense of individuality. For this reason Afro-Americans have not sought to transform the multicultural context of America into a monolithic ethos of African cultural forms. They have always recognized that their multicultural resources in America have much to offer the world; as Du Bois said, "[black] blood has a message for the world."[8] Afro-Americans simply want to enjoy authentic self-consciousness without being either ignored by the majority social group or excluded from economic opportunities.

Anglo Upward Mobility

During the colonial period in America the majority of the English-speaking persons lived in New England and Virginia. The Dutch and Swedes resided primarily in the Hudson and Delaware river valleys. German persons located in Pennsylvania. After the great wave of immigration between 1829 and 1860 many of the Irish settled in New York, Pennsylvania, and New England; a great portion of the German population settled in the Mississippi and Ohio valleys. A large percentage of the Dutch population settled in New York, Michigan, Iowa, and Wisconsin; and Norwegians located in Wisconsin and Minnesota.[9]

Between 1820 and 1920, the Germans constituted the largest single group to immigrate to America. During those years approximately 6.2 million Germans were admitted to America. Following this group in size came the Italians (consisting of about 5 million). From the Austrian and Russian sections of the world came over 8 million Poles, Jews, Hungarians, Bohemians, Slovaks, Ukrainians, and Ruthenians. About 3 million persons came from the Balkans and Asia Minor. They consisted of Greeks, Macedonians, Croatians, Albanians, Syrians, and Armenians. Two million came from Scandinavia.[10]

The immigration process can be divided into three major periods: 1820–60 represents the influx of Scots, Irish, Welsh, and Germans; 1860–90 is characterized by the influx of Prussians, Saxons, Bohemians, and Scandinavians; and 1890–1940 represents the influx of Mediterranean and Slavic persons. The peak of immigration was between 1901 and 1910, when approximately 8.8 million immigrants came to the United States.[11]

The early stage of immigration, from 1820 to 1860, was characterized by segregated pluralism. Each ethnic group tended to inhabit a particular geographical area. As immigration accelerated, ethnic neighborhoods proliferated, creating "a mosaic of segregated peoples." Most settled in urban areas. Because of their low income, education level, and skills, they settled near the central business districts of the cities. Social analysts assert that these areas consisted of enclaves of self-imposed segregation within deteriorating ghettos. But as the group acquired more education and better occupations, which helped them to move up the socioeconomic ladder, they moved to improved residential areas outside the city. One immigrant social group would then replace another. Accordingly, the pattern was duplicated by each succeeding immigrant group.

As these immigrants settled in America they surrounded themselves with community boundaries in order to maintain distinct cultural identities in language, values, customs, and traditions. But as they became more successful economically, better educated, and better acquainted with the culture of the more heterogeneous larger community, these ethnic immigrant social groups put less emphasis on the need to maintain a totally homogeneous ethnic tradition.[12]

With the second wave of immigration, between 1860 and 1890, came an increase in the number of different ethnic groups coming to America and with this a decline in the old pattern of each ethnic group creating for itself geographical boundaries.[13]

However, when we examine large urban areas from the perspective of the Afro-American, we discover a radically different story. Unlike other immigrants, Afro-Americans never chose to segregate themselves in urban ghettos. For the masses of Afro-Americans, consignment to slums was imposed systemically through discrimination. A physical feature of Afro-Americans — their skin pigmentation — restricted their upward social mobility.

The Present Color-line of Invasion and Succession

The color-line separation that existed initially for African immigrants continues to exist for the Afro-American, even for the successful and well-educated person with financial security. The fact that he or she is black summons forces of discrimination, racism, and opposition from whites. Although in many urban areas a few Afro-Americans tend to live successfully in predominantly white residential areas, it is not so for the masses of Afro-Americans. The pattern of invasion and succession has demonstrated over and over again the reality of the "white flight" — as Afro-Americans move into predominantly white neighborhoods in increasingly large numbers, whites tend to move out.[14] The pattern of invasion and succession continues to consign the masses of Afro-Americans to urban ghettos and rat-infested slums.

One's economic level determines where one lives as well as the quality of one's life: medical care, life-style, food. People's economic level in large measure depends upon the type of occupations they have or have access to. Many members of ethnic minority social groups are not able to cross the poverty line. They are blocked by the color-line, an impediment many whites forget to acknowledge. Many whites today not only exaggerate their own rapid ascent above the poverty line, they often put forth their experience as a model by which to judge the poverty-stricken situation of many oppressed ethnic minority social groups. What they fail to realize is that they were not hindered by the color-line. Often their skin color has served as an asset rather than a liability. In other words, American society has yet to judge persons by their character rather than by the color of their skin.

The Melting Pot

Not only has the Anglo-American social group remained the predominant social force in American society, but it has also been the principal shaper of America's original national consciousness. Within this context, the melting pot theory was institutionalized as the accepted standard for acculturation and assimilation. While Anglo conformity has been the goal of assimilation, the melting pot theory has played the role of means.[15]

The phrase originated with Israel Zangwill's 1908 play, *The Melting Pot*. Zangwill, an English Jew, coined the phrase for America as a metaphor for transformation by adapting it from its traditional usage in England. Subsequently, this popular term has been used almost exclusively to refer to ethnicity and intergroup relations.[16]

When the melting pot idea became incorporated into the American ideology, it encouraged immigrants to abandon their cultural backgrounds and become amalgamated into the American society. This idea functioned to explain to immigrants why they should leave behind their traditional cultural forms and should receive new ones from the American way of life. In America, all peoples were being melted or transformed into a new race of humanity, whose labors, posterity, and superiority would one day enhance the world.[17]

The idea of a new race emerging in humanity as a result of the melting pot had reached its peak of influence among scholars in 1893 when Frederick Jackson Turner, a historian from Wisconsin, presented a paper entitled "The Significance of the Frontier in American History" to the American Historical Association meeting in Chicago. Turner contended that the prevailing influence in shaping American institutions was not the European heritage but rather the experiences created by the Western frontier. This frontier, he argued, acted as a solvent for the heritages and separatist tendencies of the many nationalities that had joined the Western movement.

Turner felt that the frontier produced an Americanized, liberated, and amalgamated race that was new and different.[18]

The Problem of Resistant Superiority

Perhaps one could lament, "if only the melting pot had worked." Yet resistance to it as the means of assimilation emerged — and continues to emerge — on all sides. This functioned to promote Anglo conformity all the more.

It is important to note that while there is no scientific basis for evaluating a particular social group or culture in terms of superiority or inferiority, distortions and myths about superiority and inferiority perpetuate barriers between majority and minority social groups in America. Although many members of each social group are able to overcome this problem, racial fears, prejudices, and stereotypes persist in race relations in America. This problem has its roots in the melting pot theory and the early formation of a national consciousness in America.

For example, in 1916 Madison Grant published a book entitled *The Passing of the Great Race*, in which he argued that since superior cultures are produced by superior races and inferior cultures are produced by inferior races, the way to ensure America as a "pure" race is to keep inferior "races" such as blacks, yellows, Catholics, Jews, Poles, Slavs, and others from becoming assimilated. "Only members of the 'Aryan' or 'Nordic' [that is, English and German] races were capable of assimilating. 'Mongrel' peoples would not pollute the race."[19]

W. E. B. Du Bois in his penetrating study *The World and Africa* documents that in the early development of race consciousness in Western civilization the white race was viewed as "pure" and superior. The black race was believed to share in deception and cowardice, much of this resulting from the notion that the color black was inferior. The mixture of races was thought to be the basic cause of degradation and failure in civilization. "Everything great, everything fine, everything really successful in human culture, was white."[20]

As early as the 1890s social groups organized to champion the superiority of the white Anglo-Saxon Protestant race. Two of them were known as the Daughters of the American Revolution and the Ku Klux Klan. This surprises most Americans who think that the Ku Klux Klan originally was a white protectionist social group in the South after the Civil War. David Chalmers makes the interesting point in *Hooded Americanism* that, while the old Ku Klux Klan was anti-black, the new Klan was reborn as an unparalleled political force between 1915 and 1924. This new Klan promoted anti-black, anti-Catholic, anti-Jew, anti-communist, anti-anarchist, and anti-foreigner sentiments. It ceased to be an exclusively Southern organization. It spread throughout the United States, with some of its strongest support in the Northeast.[21]

The Solution of Anglo Conformity

American society has strongly embraced the melting pot theory because of its presupposed compatibility with Anglo conformity. One reason why America had an open-door immigration policy during the first three quarters of the nineteenth century was the belief that all immigrants could be absorbed into a focus of amalgamation and homogeneity.[22]

Zangwill's play, for example, is about an idealistic young Jewish immigrant to America, whose goal is the construction of a large American symphony in which ethnic social groups will divest themselves of their ancient cultural distinctions and become fused into one social group. An illustration of the melting pot ideology can be found in the following quotations from Zangwill's drama:

America is God's crucible, the great Melting Pot where all the races of Europe are melting and re-forming! Here you stand, good folk, think I, when I see them at Ellis Island, here you stand in your fifty groups, with your fifty languages and histories, and your fifty blood hatreds and rivalries. But you won't be long like that, brothers, for these are the fires of God you've come to — these are the fires of God. A fig for your feuds and vendettas! Germans and Frenchmen, Irishmen and

Englishmen, Jews and Russians — into the Crucible with you all! God is making the American. . . .

Yes, East and West, and North and South, the palm and the pine, the pole and the equator, the crescent and the cross — how the great Alchemist melts and fuses them with his purging flame! Here shall they all unite to build the Republic of Man and the Kingdom of God.[23]

But this great fire-fusion of all races into a new, reformed race has not occurred. It is true that many white ethnics who would usually be associated with minority social groups have succeeded in blending into the Anglo-American majority; they have been able to overcome forms of discrimination and oppression that their foreparents experienced originally in America. They have been able to move successfully up the socioeconomic ladder.

It is also true that some white ethnics have become so assimilated into the melting pot that they do not consciously identify with any particular ethnic minority social group. These white ethnics have lost their sense of minority social group identity: They have become Anglo-American culturally and physically, identifying solely with the majority social group. Thus, not only did some whites lose their ethnic physical features through intermarriage but they also acquired totally the values, mores, language, and cultural norms of the majority social group.[24]

But without this similarity of pigmentation, assimilation has not occurred. For Afro-Americans and some of the other nonwhite ethnic minority groups that have not been susceptible to blending into the melting pot, the dissimilarity of color continues to work against them. It is manifested through institutional racism and subtle forms of discrimination. This prevents them from experiencing complete assimilation.

The Decline of WASPism?

Some social analysts — William Greenbaum, Nathan Glazer, Daniel Moynihan, Peter J. Perkinson, Peter Schrag, and Nicholas Appleton — argue that white Anglo-Saxon Protestantism and the beliefs upon which it was constructed are declining in America. They suggest that the time is ripe for America to consider cultural pluralism.[25] The evidence for this argument is the increasing sense of ethnic consciousness that is modifying traditional approaches to assimilation. I maintain, however, that the melting pot ideology reflected in the manner of Anglo conformity continues to predominate in society. It continues to make social justice problematic for oppressed social groups because it encourages discrimination and institutional racism. Thus, before American society can deal effectively with the phenomenon of pluralism it has to overcome institutional racism in all of its cultural forms. William Greenbaum gives five plausible definitions of the majority social group that can help clarify for us the meaning of the phrase "majority-minority relations": (1) white Protestants who constituted approximately half of the population as of 1970; (2) white Protestants and non-Protestants who accept mainstream values; (3) the old Americans that descended from pre-1970 American families; (4) upper-class Protestants as defined by professional status; and (5) Episcopalians and Presbyterians, two of the most powerful Protestant denominations.[26]

Greenbaum attempts to show how the emerging new ethnic consciousness changes the meaning of pluralism in America. The new ethnic consciousness, he contends, represents a shift in the basis of pluralism from white Anglo-Saxon Protestantism to minority social group identification. Already in his five definitions one can see a mixture of substantive, referential, and socioeconomic bases. While I find his argument to be insightful, the critical question that needs to be raised is, What is the degree to which minority social group participation is allowed within the majority context? To a large extent, I would maintain, these minority social groups — particularly Afro-Americans, Mexican Americans, and American Indians — continue to be marginalized members of the larger society. What I take from Greenbaum's definitions is that the majority social groups in America are the physical descendants of assimilated whites and those who identify with this group, either because of their referential values or socioeconomic underpinnings.

From Ethnic to Minority

The sociologist Arnold W. Green defines an ethnic minority social group as "a foreign-stock segment of the population which preserves in some degree a distinctive way of life, in language, mannerism, habit, loyalty and the like."[27] Historical memory is important to an ethnic group. One belongs to an ethnic group not only involuntarily by birth and inculturation but also by choice. Ethnic memory refers to the impressions, patterns of behavior, expectations, and life-style that influence a person's behavior.[28]

To maintain this distinctiveness, ethnic groups are willingly cast as noticeable minority groups. The trade-off is clear: minority groups have a viable but subordinate status within the larger society. The distinctive minority characteristics are undesirable to the majority social group. The majority social group discriminates against the distinguishing characteristics. This reinforces the shared interest on the part of ethnic minority groups. Members of minority groups frequently tend to marry members of the same group. Minority group membership is acquired at birth and transmitted to future generations through acculturation and assimilation.[29] The distinctive physical or cultural characteristics give rise to the minority group's perception that it is an object of discrimination.[30] All of these factors lead to my claim that the melting pot ideology encourages discrimination and institutional racism.

The List of Minority Social Groups

The phrase "minority social group" now includes all groups that have been kept from full participation in the American mainstream because of discrimination. This means that women are to be included among the list of those victimized by discrimination: Afro-Americans, American Indians, Asian Americans, Jews, Latinos, Mexican Americans, Puerto Ricans, and so forth.

There was a time when "minority social group" referred primarily to Afro-Americans and American Indians. But since the black power revolution in the 1960s, other minorities have discovered a new sense of ethnic consciousness, and now the phrase is used more inclusively. The phrase also refers to those groups that tend to define their cultural identity differently from the social norms or archetypes[31] prescribed by the majority social group.

The Modern Scientific World View and Human Oppression

We have seen how the idea of Anglo conformity and the melting pot perpetuated, in the early formation of America's national consciousness, the interest of the majority social group, thereby relegating oppressed minority social groups to marginal status. My purpose now is to show how this idea found fresh inspiration in the beliefs and metaphysical presuppositions upon which the modern scientific world view was constructed. It is my contention that the presuppositions present in the modern world view not only reinforced the quest for power, control, wealth, and a leisure life-style but were used as a rationale for the exploitation of both human and natural resources.

Process philosophers have frequently shown how the beliefs and presuppositions present in this modern world view have contributed to the exploitation of natural resources.[32] But they have not demonstrated sufficiently how these beliefs and presuppositions have reinforced the exploitation and depersonalization of minority social groups.

Along with an analysis of the social implications of these issues, I will point to the philosophical and theological inadequacies present in traditional approaches to pluralism. There is a close kinship between the development of scientific theory, metaphysics, theological discourse, and social philosophy. All academic disciplines, for example, usually adhere to the accepted beliefs, truths, or presuppositions present in the prevailing natural science of a particular time. We will see not only how the Newtonian paradigm has influenced all dimensions of knowledge for several centuries but also how its presuppositions have reinforced minority group oppression.

I might insert here that Sir Isaac Newton himself (1642–1727) was probably not a Newtonian. For him to be a Newtonian would mean that he endorsed the many applications of his system of thought that followed in the centuries after him. "The Newtonians in the century after the master's death," states George S. Brett, "went so far in their exaggeration of his principles that they could not even understand how Newton himself was about to reconcile science and religion."[33] Disciples, in applying the master's principles, usually become either left- or right-wing interpreters. The more radical left-wing interpreters modify the thinker's system. The conservative and orthodox right-wing interpreters maintain more consistency with the original ideas.

The Newtonian Paradigm and Its Implications

The presuppositions of the Newtonian paradigm brought a radical dimension to theological discourse by repudiating the ancient division of the world into two planes, the celestial and the terrestrial, and establishing the idea of one law in the universe. This gave rise to the notion that the concept of God and the idea of law were not antagonistic. But these presuppositions also took quite a conservative turn when applied to social, political, and economic systems. Our discussion will critique the conservative dimensions.

"Paradigm" here describes a body of knowledge, a set of beliefs, presuppositions, or accepted truths that govern the lives of persons for centuries. All cultural expressions, including conceptions of God, morality, customs, politics, economics, and education, are shaped by the existing paradigm.

Paradigms are based on the prevailing natural science,[34] and, as I have mentioned, all other academic disciplines usually adhere to the presuppositions undergirding scientific paradigms. Because accepted truths of paradigms become institutionalized in social structures, it is always difficult for society to accept new truths based on different understandings of reality.

There are two basic reasons why it is imperative for us to examine the philosophical, theological, and social aspects of the Newtonian paradigm. First, the Newtonian paradigm prevailed as the predominant ethos in all forms of knowledge for several centuries. Because the Newtonian paradigm held sway when European nations and the

United States began to seek power and control of human and natural resources during the modern period, we need to see now how its presuppositions bolstered the quest for wealth on the part of the majority social group and sustained the oppression of minority social groups.

Second, such an examination will help us to see more clearly why the Newtonian model fails to provide the means for successful majority-minority intergroup relations. If we do not identify these inadequacies, we run the risk of perpetuating them in new models of pluralism.

Newton's Metaphysical Shortcomings

As an intellectual of rare magnitude, Newton enjoys the extraordinary distinction of having become an authority — paralleled only by Aristotle — in an age that opposes authority. The supremacy and authority that Newton's ideas acquired in the development of modern science remain unquestioned. In describing ultimate matters of fact, however, Newton's approach remains much too uncritical. Although Newton was a genius in scientific discovery, in areas of metaphysics, philosophy, and theology, he simply took over the presuppositions of his intellectual ancestry — formulating them systematically, updating them occasionally, and remolding them slightly into a style more compatible with his particular extra-scientific interest, to be sure, but accepting them nevertheless without fundamentally questioning them.[35]

This is one of the reasons why Whitehead critiqued the foundations of seventeenth-century science and philosophy. "The truth is that science started its modern career by taking over ideas derived from the weakest side of the philosophies of Aristotle's successors," wrote Whitehead.[36]

In fact, the emerging new ethnic consciousness represents a reaction against the inadequacies of traditional approaches to pluralism. Unless these inadequacies are exposed, we may be lulled into accepting their viability and merely reformulating them into our new models. The only way we can ensure sound alternatives for human liberation is to embrace the self-critical perspective. Perpetuating antiquated models of pluralism will do nothing but impede liberation for both majority and minority groups. Our approach must both negate and transform traditional models, and we must not allow these alternative approaches to become merely the tool of the majority social group.

David Tracy has earnestly appealed to us to employ both negation and transformation in approaching traditional models of liberation.

> In place of liberating symbols which can include the protest of the oppressed, the memory of their suffering, the demand for the negation of their oppression, and the radical affirmation of the possibilities of personal and societal liberation, one finds instead demystified, reified, impoverished symbols of a conformist development which effectively insure — as they are articulated at the level of mass-culture — the continued domination of the developed powers in modern technological society.[37]

As we build upon the enormous contributions of the Western heritage, we must be willing to repudiate its shortcomings while at the same time affirming its strengths. To a great extent, the viability of traditional models is measured by their capacity to relate to the ever-changing demands of the human predicament. Whitehead recognizes this when he says, "In its turn every philosophy will suffer a deposition. But the bundle of philosophic systems expresses a variety of general truths about the universe, awaiting coordination and assignment of their various spheres of validity. Such progress in coordination is provided by the advance of philosophy; and in this sense philosophy has advanced from Plato onwards."[38]

The Mechanistic View of Nature

Fundamental to the formation of the modern scientific world view was a generally accepted belief in the mechanistic theory of nature, often referred to as scientific materialism. Its basic presuppositions can be found in every discipline — modern literature, religion, social philosophies, politics, economics.[39] These presuppositions had profound consequences for every aspect of modern culture. The philosophy of scientific materialism culminated in the Newtonian paradigm, which describes the world as a machine. Building upon René Descartes's foundation, Newton did two important things: he discovered the mathematical method and described mechanical motion. And he applied the method universally. Newton brought Descartes's dream into reality. Namely, he arrived at a comprehensive mechanical interpretation of the world by using the mathematical, deductive process.[40]

The Newtonian paradigm represents a systematic synthesis of the Copernican and the Cartesian revolutions. Newton put into systematic form the mechanical view of nature.[41] Since Newton applied the mechanical interpretation of nature to all forms of existence, he formulated the principles of mechanical science into a cosmology.

Cosmology is a branch of metaphysics that deals with the origin and structure of the world. The study of cosmology is integral to investigating world views. Metaphysicians attempt to make their cosmologies consistent with the prevailing natural science. Newton made scientific materialism consistent with what can be referred to as classical physics. And Whitehead, as we will see, developed a metaphysical system consistent with quantum mechanics and relativity theory.

Scholars in the humanistic, natural, social, and behavioral sciences alike are deeply indebted to Whitehead (1861–1947) for his monumental achievement in exposing the inadequacies present in the Newtonian paradigm. In order to construct an organic model of pluralism based on quantum mechanics and relativity theory, Whitehead realized that he had to repudiate the metaphysical deficiencies of seventeenth-century science. His achievement enabled philosophers and theologians to succeed in developing a metaphysical system based on genuine pluralism.

Although Whitehead pioneered in constructing a metaphysic of pluralism, there is an urgent need for scholars to go a step further. We need to think through the implications of Whitehead's model of organic pluralism for majority-minority intergroup relations. Such is the task of this book.

Whitehead's theoretical critique of the Newtonian paradigm incited a revolution in metaphysics. Because Western culture had so thoroughly adapted scientific materialism, an alternative conceptualization had been unimaginable.[42]

Although the origin of scientific materialism in Western thought predated the systematic formulation of the philosophy of substance, it derived its meaning from that philosophy. The original thinkers attributed with shaping scientific materialism are pre-Socratic philosophers, known as the pluralists. They were cosmologists, meaning that their primary focus was on the origin, nature, and structure of the world. Along with speculating about the origin of the world, they attempted to account for the multiplicity of things in the world on the one hand, and the oneness of reality on the other hand.

The two pluralists noted for developing scientific materialism are Leucippus and Democritus. Scientific materialism is based on the atomic theory. The ancient philosophers believed that the world is made of a multiplicity of atoms, which are solid, irreducible, indivisible, and eternal. It was believed that these atoms had no beginning or end. They had no need of an external force to put them in motion. These atoms, in different shapes and sizes, were mechanistic and naturalistic. Although Leucippus and Democritus made no acute distinction between mind and matter, it is appropriate to say that they maintained a materialistic view of the world in that they believed that irreducible bits of matter contained the final stuff of existence.

In the Newtonian paradigm the materialist world view was made more complex with the emergence of the scientific method, the birth of technology, the development of modern mathematics, and a systematic formulation of the idea of substantialism. (I am using "substantialism" to mean that the basic unit of reality in the Newtonian paradigm consisted of unchanging matter. This matter was referred to as substances. Although the philosophy of substance in its technical meaning is usually associated with Aristotle's metaphysics, it exists in modified forms throughout the history of Western philosophy and theology.)

Advocates of dualistic philosophies contended that the world consists of two substances, matter and mind. Those attracted to monistic philosophies argued that the world is made up of one fundamental substance, which is God. And pluralistic philosophies, which were based on scientific materialism, conceived the world as consisting of many self-contained individual substances.

Consequently, whether one incorporates the idea of substantialism into a dualistic or monistic framework, its basic premise makes genuine pluralism impossible in metaphysics. Examples of this can be seen in the philosophies of Descartes, Spinoza, and Newton.

From Descartes and Spinoza to Newton

René Descartes (1596–1650), who is referred to as the father of modern philosophy, invented analytic geometry and made important contributions to the development of psychology, physics, and astronomy. He distinguished himself as a philosopher with the publication of three works: *Discourse on Method, Meditations,* and *Principles of Philosophy.* Using his famous criterion of truth *cogito ergo sum* (I think, therefore I am), Descartes employed the category of doubt to verify the existence of the self. He held that a thing that doubts is a thing that exists. Since the individual engages in doubting, the process itself verifies the existence of the self, because to doubt is to think and to think is to exist. Without the existence of the self there could be no doubting or thinking. Consequently, Descartes concluded, the criterion of truth that is self-verifying is the thinking self.[43]

Because the idea of substantialism characterizes Descartes's dualistic framework, he views the thinking self as an independent substance. He perceives the mind as capable of existing independently of the body. He arrives at the existence of the body differently than he arrives at the existence of the mind. For Descartes it is the mind that doubts and thinks, not the body. Since the body cannot think, its existence can only be inferred. The world, therefore, is composed of two independent substances, one mental and the other physical. Descartes considers the mind and the body to be the two primary substances; since the nature of a substance is its attributes, mind and body manifest themselves in the world through different modes of activity containing mental and physical dimensions. Descartes perceives all physical objects in the external world to be manifestations of a physical substance. Although Descartes argues that God is the only pure substance capable of existing independently, he defines mental and physical substances in such a manner that each becomes autonomous.

And, whereas Descartes starts the criterion of truth verification with an analysis of the thinking self, using the deductive method he makes dualism characteristic of all existence. Whitehead recognizes that when dualism is perceived as a description of ultimate matters of fact, it distorts the nature of reality. Cartesian dualism creates in metaphysics a fundamental gulf between the spiritual and the physical dimensions of existence. This notion, as we will see, has had devastating effects in majority-minority intergroup relations. It reinforced the manner in which the Western section of the world exploited nature, enslaved Afro-Americans, and dehumanized American Indians.

The philosophy of dualism tends to put forms of reality over against each other; it fails to create a context for mutuality, supportiveness, openness, and receptivity. Cartesian dualism functions as a closed system; the mental and the physical are self-contained. They lack a sense of social relatedness, which is imperative for genuine pluralism.

Although the philosopher Benedict Spinoza (1632–1677) developed a monistic system as a corrective to Cartesian dualism, because Spinoza integrated the prevailing idea of substantialism into his metaphysical system he was not able to formulate a pluralistic model capable of overcoming the perception of the real as an unchanging substance. When Descartes divided substances into two kinds, the mind as the primary representative of a thinking substance and the body as the primary representative of an extended substance, he made the error of making them exclusive of each other.[44] While it is true that Descartes made an effort to show how the mind and body interact,[45] Spinoza found his conclusion unsatisfactory. Spinoza attempted to correct Descartes by arguing that there is one fundamental substance. Consequently, what we experience in the realms of mental and physical processes is not the manifestation of two independent substances. To the contrary, Spinoza suggests the mental and the physical are two distinct aspects of the same process. This one reality is what he describes as substance. He defines substance as that which is self-contained, conceived of itself, and does not need to be formed from the conception of anything else.

Based on Spinoza's definition of substance, God or the world is the only category capable of existing independently. Substance alone is self-sufficient. Everything else in the world depends upon it, but it does not depend upon anything else. Substance manifests itself through attributes and modes. The essence of substance consists of its attributes. Since the nature of substance means that it is infinite, Spinoza believed substance must possess an infinite number of attributes. However, only two of these attributes are known to humanity. They are the mental and physical dimensions.

These attributes manifest themselves through modes. The plurality of things in the world, which we perceive through sense perception, Spinoza ascribes to modes. The word *mode* designates a modification of substance, meaning that a mode is conceived by something else. All finite things in the world are dependent upon the one substance, which Spinoza identifies as God or the world.

The idea that all things are identified with God as a substance and that God does not exist separate from the world qualifies Spinoza's system as a form of monism. He identifies God and the world as one substance. The word associated with Spinoza's view of God is *pantheism.*

For Spinoza God is the efficient cause of everything in the world. In other words, all finite expressions are merely manifestations of the nature of God. All things come from God's nature by necessity. Implied in Spinoza's doctrine of God is absolute determinism — the cause of all finite things in the world is necessarily determined by God.[46]

On the one hand Whitehead considers Spinoza's philosophy of monism a significant advancement beyond the dualistic framework of Descartes. But on the other hand he realizes the necessity of avoiding the idea of substantialism, which was a major stumbling block for both Descartes and Spinoza.

The philosophies of Descartes and Spinoza are inadequate for a metaphysic of pluralism. Descartes's mind-body split, which is the classic form of dualism characteristic of the Newtonian paradigm, is inadequate in that it individualizes reality into mutually exclusive categories. Such a tendency compartmentalizes the final acts of experience and functions contrary to pluralism. In Spinoza's monism all finite expressions of reality are dissolved into collectivity and sameness. It is contrary to individuality, which is a prerequisite for pluralism. The notion of substantialism, which characterized Descartes's dualism and Spinoza's monism, is also contrary to pluralism.

Newton failed to advance the quest for pluralism beyond the inadequacies present in Descartes and Spinoza. His view of reality was also based on the principle of substantialism. The Newtonian materialist cosmology distorted the final acts of experience. Whitehead says that it treated the abstract as though it were the concrete. He describes this distortion as the "fallacy of misplaced concreteness," which occurs when abstract aspects of experience are interpreted as though they are the real. The materialist cosmology interpreted the final acts of experience as irreducible bits of matter spread throughout space in a configuration. These bits of matter possessed only external relations.

Whitehead says, "To say that a bit of matter has simple location means that, in expressing its spatio-temporal relations, it is adequate to state that it is where it is, in a definite finite region of space, and throughout a definite finite duration of time apart from any essential reference of the relations of that bit of matter to other regions of space and to other durations of time."[47] In itself this material, the final acts of experience, was senseless, valueless, and purposeless. These bits of matter were thought to follow a fixed routine imposed by external relations.[48]

Now, let us turn our discussion to identifying some of the presuppositions and beliefs that were present in the Newtonian paradigm and that reinforced some forms of oppression experienced by minority social groups.

The Modern Institution of Slavery

Slavery and the Newtonian Paradigm's Understanding of Individualism and Nature

First, the idea of thoroughgoing individualism needs to be considered. The Newtonian paradigm is individualistic from beginning to end. Each bit of matter was thought to be separate, autonomous, independent, and self-contained. Reality did not contain internal relatedness. Rather, each form of reality was highly individualized and mechanized, meaning that it functioned based on absolute space-time. Nothing is more characteristic of modern humanity than a preoccupation with individualism.

This newly found individualism meant the abandonment of all forms of authoritarianism. No longer did the church possess final authority in questions of morality, as was the case during the medieval period; rather, each individual was endowed with the freedom to determine moral standards. This included reading and interpreting the Bible based on one's own conscience.

The Protestant reformers, Martin Luther, John Calvin, John Knox, and Zwingli, contributed to the birth of this individualism. Although this idea did not originate with the Protestant Reformation — from the thirteenth century and earlier there existed "within the church tendencies toward simplification, individualism and salvation without external sacraments"[49] — it reached unprecedented acceptance during the Protestant Reformation.

The forces let loose by the Newtonian paradigm amplified this sense of individualism. Other developments furthered it as well: the revival of nominalism, the Copernican revolution, the scientific method, and the emergence of such philosophical systems as rationalism, naturalism, subjectivism, empiricism, and idealism.

The ethos of the modern period, then, with its belief in knowledge as power and the Commercial Revolution's emphasis on the acquisition of wealth, granted permission for the modern institution of slavery and the slave trade. The idea of individualism was taken to the extreme. It bordered on licentiousness and anarchy. "It was the freedom to destroy freedom, the freedom of some to exploit the rights of others. It was, indeed, the concept of freedom with little or no social responsibility. If, then, a man was determined to be free, who was there to tell him that he was not entitled to enslave others?"[50]

Concurrently the economies of Europe and the United States experienced a revitalization. Commercial activities burgeoned. A new awareness of the power of capital contributed to the breakdown of feudalism and the development of towns. The Commercial Revolution thus heightened competition among merchants.

This competition manifested itself through ruthless exploitation of any commodity, including human beings, that could foster economic gain. It was this very spirit that was behind the development of the modern institution of slavery.[51] To American society the slave trade meant power, wealth, leisure, and the control of resources.

Second, let us consider the Newtonian paradigm's perception of nature. Nature was believed to be soundless, scentless, colorless, and meaningless.[52] It is no wonder that domination and manipulation of the environment have been characteristic of the modern period. This license to coerce nature to meet human need and greed is the same one the Newtonian paradigm granted to those who wished to coerce human beings into slavery.

This link between the coercion of nature and the coercion of human beings was glaringly revealed in the rationale offered for enslaving Africans and bringing them to America, and that link focused around the issue of color. "Blackness," like nature, was viewed as inferior and thus offered license for coercion. The immense and long-range ramifications of this coercion based on color have extended through centuries of American history and on into the present day. In *The Souls of Black Folk*, W. E. B. Du Bois touched upon these issues, writing: "The problem of the twentieth century is the problem of the color-line, the relation of the lighter races of men in Asia and Africa, in America and the islands of the sea. It was a phase of this problem that caused the Civil War."[53] Just as it was necessary to designate nature as meaningless in order to coerce and degrade it, so it was necessary to associate blackness with degradation and inferiority in order to justify slavery. Africans were considered barbarians, half human. Because whites perceived themselves as superior and blacks inferior, the word *Negro* associated blackness with slavery and degradation.[54] The deportation of Africans and their enslavement in America were justified as a means of "humanizing" them. And in the assimilation process Afro-Americans were denied the use of their native language, their family structure was torn asunder, and they were forced to adopt the cultural expression of the majority social group.[55]

The Citizenship Issue

Since Afro-Americans were thought to be a commodity to be bought and sold, they were excluded from the whites' view of human experience. "We hold these truths to be self-evident; that all men are created equal; that they are endowed by their creator with certain unalienable rights; that among these are life, liberty, and the pursuit of happiness"[56] excluded Afro-Americans because they were considered half human.

The Dred Scott Decision of 1857 is another example of this pervasive prejudice. Dred Scott was a slave from Missouri. In 1834 Scott's master, an army surgeon, took him into the free state of Illinois to live. Later he was taken into what is now Minnesota. In these parts of the country slavery was prohibited by the Missouri Compromise of 1820. Scott was then brought back to Missouri and sold to another army surgeon. In 1853 Scott filed a suit in a federal court in Missouri on the grounds that he was a free man. He contended that because he was taken into a free territory he was free upon his return to Missouri.

Scott's slave master, a New York citizen, argued that Scott could not bring a lawsuit in a federal court because Scott was not a citizen. The two issues to be resolved by the court were to establish whether Scott was in reality a citizen of Missouri and also whether being taken into free territory made Scott a free man. The latter issue involved a decision as to whether Congress had the power under the Constitution to prohibit slavery in the free territory of Minnesota. Chief Justice Taney's decision, which was supported by the majority members in the court, was that Congress did not have power to prohibit slavery, making the Missouri Compromise unconstitutional. Therefore, in March 1857 the Supreme Court ruled that Dred Scott and all other "people of African descent are not and cannot be citizens of the United States, and cannot sue in any of the United States courts." In rendering this decision, the Supreme Court, the highest judicial body of the land, concluded that Afro-Americans were inferior and unfit to function on an equal basis with the white normative social group. Consequently, they had no rights that whites were bound to respect. The decision gave final confirmation to the prevailing belief that "under the Constitution and Government of the United States, [Afro-Americans] are nothing, and can be nothing but an alien, disenfranchised and degraded class."[57]

During the deliberations a question was raised as to whether Afro-Americans were citizens originally upon the adoption of the Constitution of the United States. Or, to put it another way, did the original shapers of the Constitution intend to include Afro-Americans? Taney gave an unequivocal response:

> Can a negro whose ancestors were imported into this country, sold as slaves, become a member of the political community formed and brought into existence by the Constitution of the United States, and as such become entitled to all rights, privileges, and immunities, guaranteed by the instrument to the citizen? One of which rights is the privilege of suing in a court of the United States in the cases specified in the Constitution.... The only matter in issue before the court therefore, is whether the descendants of such slaves, when they shall be emancipated, or who are born of parents who had become free before their birth, are citizens of a state, in the sense in which the word "citizen" is used in the Constitution of the United States.[58]

Taney's conclusion was that Afro-Americans were not citizens within the original intention of the Constitution, that their status throughout the United States upon the adoption of the Constitution was noncitizenship. Although there were some free Afro-Americans at that time, none was considered a citizen. It is important to note that the decision of Chief Justice Taney was characteristic of how the entire nation viewed Afro-Americans.[59]

God and Culture in Paradox: A Critique of Traditional Theism

My attempt here is not to give an exhaustive appraisal of the Newtonian paradigm's perception of God's role in history; I want only to show some of the ways in which that perception has been used in history to sustain oppression.

Traditional theism in the modern period dredged a deep gulf between God and the world. Modern theists, including Newton, believed that God — from a transcendent abode — created the world as a great machine, set it going, and occasionally corrected it when it malfunctioned. One of God's important tasks was to maintain with accuracy the mathematical regularity of the world. Things in the world were thought to function deterministically, based on God's prescribed design. Motion, change, and all activity were believed to follow certain laws of nature. Inherent in this theism is a dualism that presupposes the existence of a supernaturalistic structure that has a restricted and highly categorized relation with the natural order.[60]

We have inherited this dualism and perpetuate its divisiveness when we speak of, for example, sacred-secular, spirit-matter, soul-body, interiority-exteriority, infinity-finite, being-becoming, eternal-temporal, one-many, good-bad, light-dark. Because traditional theists tended to compartmentalize God's relation to the world, they perceived God's intervention in the world much too narrowly.

This narrow perception inevitably fostered provincialism and ethnocentrism. Paul Tillich was one who understood the ramifications of such provincialism and who foresaw that this provincialism would clash with the expanding pluralism in the United States and the world. Anticipating the impact of pluralism on modernity, Tillich envisioned the need for contemporary humanity to resist provincialism. He poses the question: "Will America remain what it has been to us, a country in which people from every country can overcome their spiritual provincialism?"[61] He concludes by suggesting our efforts should be geared toward "resisting and conquering provincialism, including theological and philosophical provincialism."[62]

Tillich, then, understood the deep-seated causes and problems of such a narrow and provincial vision. One of the fundamental problems of this provincial vision had to do with the way in which the supernaturalists or traditional theists (both terms refer here to a similar perception) conceived of the nature of God: they made the error of conceiving the nature of God in a way that made God an exception to all metaphysical principles. In other words, those categories that the supernaturalists ascribed to God, they did not ascribe to the world.[63] Their conception made God eminently real and the world derivatively real. In attempting to surmount this impasse between God and the world, Whitehead says, "God is not to be treated as an exception to all metaphysical principles, invoked to save their collapse. He is their chief exemplification."[64]

Thus Tillich and Whitehead understood the problems inherent in the supernaturalist view of God and the world. Here it might be worthwhile to spell out some of these more clearly, for some grave consequences result from adhering to the supernaturalist view of God. For example, when a gulf is created between God and the world, there remains no framework to call persons to a sense of moral responsibility. Persons are not perceived as sacred. Their value, dignity, and self-worth are lost, and they are reduced to things or utility. The image of God within persons becomes dwarfed or distorted. When God is perceived as remote, separate from activities in the world, it encourages persons to separate individual moral responsibility from social justice, and moral responsibility comes to mean simply responding to God on an individual, private basis. It does not include the community. From within the supernaturalist view of God, one misses seeing that when persons are exploited, oppressed, or dehumanized the very reality of God is negatively affected. In short, the supernaturalist view fails to integrate the social and spiritual dimensions of life. For this reason it fails to foster genuine ethical responsibility.

Another grave consequence of the supernaturalist view of God has to do with eschatology. Its vision of eschatological hope is almost exclusively otherworldly. It fails to integrate the present and not-yet dimensions of the kingdom of God. Because it envisions the kingdom of God as beyond history, it fails to take the socio-cultural context seriously. Rather than focusing on transforming and redeeming the historical process, its exclusively future orientation opens up a disjunction between the historical process and the kingdom of God. Consequently, it does not lend itself to liberation and social justice.

The Monopolar God

The gulf between God and the world created by the supernaturalists can be described as a function of a monopolar conception of God. *Monopolar* means that God possessed only one experiential dimension, which was believed to be the transcendent realm. God was thought to be static, self-contained, complete, and nonrelative.[65]

Based on the monopolar conception of God, which became quite influential in certain aspects of theism and deism, early developers of supernaturalism and dualism accepted uncritically Greek philosophy's negative assessment of the pluralistic dimensions of finite existence. "Within the framework of Greek values, there was something intrinsically superior about the static and monistic and something intrinsically inferior about the dynamic and pluralistic."[66]

The monopolar idea ascribed to God such attributes as perfection, being, permanence, pure actuality, and creativity. It ascribed to the finite pluralistic dimensions such attributes as imperfection, becoming, change, potentiality, and creation. The static and monistic categories ascribed to God hold a positive value. The categories of change and imperfection ascribed to the pluralistic aspects of finite existence hold a negative value.[67]

For example, in Aristotle's metaphysics God moves the world by desire or attraction, not by becoming involved in existential history. And God, perceived as the object of attraction, moves the world by being loved. For Aristotle the love the world has for God and the self-love of God cause movement in the world. By viewing God as the uncaused cause and the unmoved mover, Aristotle attempted to avoid the problem of infinite regression.[68] But he created an enormous gulf between God and the world that has plagued traditional theism since its assimilation into Christian theology. Traditional theists have attempted to bridge this gulf by emphasizing both the transcendence and immanence of God. But they have continued to exclude finitude and temporality from God's nature.[69] Consequently, this narrow, one-sided view of God has impressed upon the Western mentality the idea that the unchanging, static, complete, and immutable realm of the transcendent is superior ontologically, because it represents the abode of God. Obversely, it has viewed the realm of finitude and temporality as inferior because it does not represent God's interpenetration.[70]

Traditional theism has influenced Western cultural heritage toward a polarization of social groups. For example, oppressors argue that God is on their side, as witnessed during the institution of slavery in America and during the civil rights struggle. In fact, Martin Luther King, Jr., is reported to have heard advocates of discrimination saying, "God is a charter member of the White Citizens Council."[71] We can see this taking place with more intensity in South Africa and Latin America. Under the sway of traditional theism, the intervention of God into history is viewed by oppressors as support for their existing political, social, and economic control. God's activity is not interpreted as counteracting the power and control of the status quo.

Oppressed minorities, on the other hand, have tried to counteract these forces of oppression by arguing that God is on their side. They maintain that since God is the architect of justice, love, mercy, and goodness, meaning that God is opposed to injustice, hatred, dehumanization, and exploitation, God's presence in the world must be on their side.[72]

Because of this, God's intervention in history is seen to legitimate all the strategies used to protest against oppression. The oppressor, by contrast, interprets God's intervention as meaning just the opposite. The oppressors argue that since cosmic laws always function deterministically and since these forces have obviously selected them to control both natural and human resources, God's occasional interventions in the world are for the sake of keeping each social group in its respective place.

Social Change and God's Will

If one follows philosophy, one would conclude that radical strategies to eradicate oppression stand contrary to the order of the cosmic economy. And whatever is opposed to the cosmic economy is opposed to the will of God. And because the natural order (and God's will) is thought to be fixed, static, attempts at change are aberrations, and thus is oppression perpetuated.

If one believes that the basic contradictions of life are fixed, final, and ultimate, defeat and pessimism reign. But if by chance one believes that these contradictions, regardless of their intensity, are not final and fixed, hope and optimism reign.

Slave masters in America taught the slaves that the apparent contradictions in life were forever binding and final. Their plight was fixed, finished, unchanging, and inescapable. By placing the slaves in such an agonizing grip of inevitables, the slave masters believed that they were obliterating any alternatives for the slaves.

For the slave masters this was a convenient social philosophy. All ideas of social superiority and racial inequality were elevated to the dimension of the natural order of things. They believed that the institution of slavery was ordained by a partial God who consigned some groups to superiority and others to inferiority.

But because the slaves never firmly believed that they were trapped in inevitables and that life's contradictions were final, they possessed hope. This hope emerged even "in the midst of the most barren and most tragic circumstances."[73] It was the complete renunciation of the thoroughgoing dualism of the modern period.

What we have here is the powerful and affluent majority social group perceiving God's intervention in the world perpetuating the debasement of minority social groups. Meanwhile, the oppressed minorities counter that the days of the powerful are numbered, because ultimately God is in complete control of history. But the polarization between majority and minority social groups cannot be abolished this way.

The traditional theistic perspective denies that God can participate in the affairs of a social group that may adhere to different ideas. And, in some instances, majority social groups have used political, ideological, and socioreligious differences as grounds for declaring war against other social groups. The thinking is that if social groups do not adhere to the prevailing ideology, they are outside the divine life and are therefore subject to negative consequences. This belief has led perpetrators of war and violence to consider themselves instruments commissioned by God to execute the divine will in the world, identifying God's purpose with their particular ideology.

This theistic bias feeds provincialism and ethnocentrism. Conformity with the majority is the measure of God's intervention in the world. Maintaining the status quo is the indication of God's activity. The imbalances and inequities between the majority and minority social groups thus become institutionalized and accepted.

They are institutionalized through large corporate structures that limit options for minority social groups and favor the majority. They are disseminated through national policies and ideologies designed to perpetuate the interests of the majority social group and ignore the marginalized minority groups. We fail to realize that when the majority develops systemic malfunctions that sustain marginal existence, it jeopardizes the whole human condition. We must recognize that the white majority, which is monopolizing human and natural resources throughout the global village, will never be free until its victims are free.

God's Participation in Culture: A Critique of Hegel's Evolutionary Theism

Alongside the inadequacies of the Newtonian deterministic view of God's role in history are those of a predeterministic interpretation of God's role in history. Both perspectives are not conducive to liberating the oppressed; they perpetuate forms of oppression. From the Hegelian perspective God preordains the course of historic events, and from the Newtonian perspective God ordains the natural order of things.

As we have seen, in the Newtonian paradigm all phenomena in the world function according to natural laws and principles determined by the cosmic process itself. In Newton's system of thought, God, of course, does not predetermine events in history; rather, God basically corrects things when they go wrong. The will of God is perceived as consistent with the natural order. Because some social groups were believed to be selected by the divine cosmic economy to control natural and human resources and other social groups were believed to be selected as subordinates, oppressors concluded that God was in support of the status quo.

The predeterministic perspective differs in the sense that all events in history become the unfolding of cosmic design, which is preordained by God. Hegel's philosophy of history is a classic illustration of predeterminism.

Hegel's Philosophy of History

While there is much that is of value in Hegel's religious philosophy, his philosophy of history contains elements that are contrary to liberating the oppressed. My purpose is not to do the type of Feuerbachian or Marxist critique of Hegel's thought that was done by left-wing Hegelians in the nineteenth century. Nor do I plan to critique the conservative dimensions of right-wing interpreters of Hegel.[74] Rather, my attempt is to show some of the negative implications present in Hegel's philosophy of history when applied to the liberating struggle that is being advanced by minority social groups.

Hegel, along with Schleiermacher, is a pivotal figure among the nineteenth-century Protestant religious philosophers who succeeded in overcoming the supernaturalism present in traditional theism. As we have seen, that theism found affinity in the Newtonian mechanistic explanation of God's role in the cosmic economy. Because the eighteenth and nineteenth centuries idealized the Newtonian explanation, thereby making Newton's *Principia* the basis of scientific experimentation, and extended its principles to all forms of knowledge, God's existence became relegated to either a deistic or a theistic approach. Hegel's contribution was to show how the principle of identity enables the reality of God to correct the errors present in both deism and traditional theism.

I pointed out that the Newtonian explanation argued that because God created the world originally as a perfect machine, the world needed only occasional supernaturalistic interventions from God to correct it. If something is created perfect and complete, it should need only occasional development whenever something needs repairing. Traditional theists tended to adhere closer to Newton's own position, which allowed for God's occasional interference in the world to make repairs. And pantheism, which is the direct opposite of both deism and theism, tended to dissolve God's existence totally into thoroughgoing immanentism. While Hegel attempted to correct the error of deism and theism, his conception of God included some of the weaknesses inherent in each. A few brief words about one of the shortcomings of deism may help to pave the way for my explanation of how Hegel's philosophy of history reinforces human oppression.

Deism is correct in its recognition that God transcends the world. It is essential for God to maintain distinct individuality and self-identity to the extent that an aspect of God's being exists beyond the world. But deism errs in concluding that transcendence exhausts the reality of God. Such a conclusion makes the reality of God totally remote to history; consequently, God becomes indifferent about creaturely existence.[75]

This is inadequate for oppressed persons because it means that God has no direct relation to their particular needs. God relates to the world only indirectly. Because God is static, God does not possess sensitivity to the needs of oppressed persons and therefore cannot make a significant difference in their situation. The existential requirement for a God that is concerned and cares about the human condition is lost in deism. God's remoteness makes God obsolete and minimizes God's value for existential history.

Freedom from Predeterminism

Although Hegel succeeds in overcoming the exclusive transcendence of deism, and he closes the gap that exists between God and the world found in traditional theism, his philosophy of history works contrary to the liberation of the oppressed. According to Hegel, all comes from God; all is in God; all is created by God; and all remains as a moment in God.[76] The problem resides in the predeterministic aspect of his thought, not in his organic conception of God. Oppressed persons cannot afford to submit themselves to all the forces of history as instances of God's preordained will, as Hegel's philosophy of history implies.

While it is constructive to view God's presence as being in a certain manner related to all events in history, because this guards against relegating God's presence exclusively to particular social groups, it is not in the interest of liberation to say, as Hegel does, that all history is the result of God's plan. For persons at the top of the socioeconomic ladder such a belief succeeds in perpetuating their self-interest and keeping oppressed social groups subordinate. It stands against the development of protest philosophies geared toward changing the course of history. For persons at the bottom of the ladder such a belief may imply that God opposes rather than supports their efforts to attain liberation.

Hegel says, "What is rational is real and what is real is rational."[77] The assumption here is that since God has predetermined the course of events in history, social structures represent the objective manifestation of God. In other words, existing social systems are partly reflective of the real. Absolute Spirit, which is God's self unfolding in history, is the truly real. And since for Hegel structures created by humankind are extensions of God, everything in the world, including the human spirit and nature, are manifestations of God.

Such a position suggests that one's goal in life should not consist of rebelling against social structures; rather, Hegel views one's goal to be that of total submission to the present course of history. What one gets in this type of social philosophy is political accommodation.[78] It reinforces the status quo. It says in reality that if one attempts to change existing structures in society, regardless of how demonic they may be, one's actions are contrary to the will of God.

Since Hegel views the state as constituting the real and because the majority social group always controls existing social structures, the implication this has for oppressed social groups becomes quite self-evident. The state does not ensure concrete freedom of all persons as Hegel suggests; it protects the concrete freedom of the majority social group, while often condoning the exploitation and political disenfranchisement of the oppressed.[79]

Hegel views history as the movement of God toward freedom. In a real sense for Hegel history is the autobiography of God. In history freedom is attained through self-consciousness, and the human spirit contains finite self-consciousness. Because Hegel sees the objective expressions of freedom realized in the community through laws, customs, and other cultural forms, he does not see the need for individuals to change their particular social circumstances in the event that their circumstances fail to cohere with the nature of freedom. For Hegel freedom is significant for the total community and the world rather than for the individual. He believes that the individual represents a finite subjective expression of freedom.

If, for example, particular individuals experience lesser degrees of freedom, Hegel feels that they should attempt to grasp just how their particular social circumstances ultimately enhance the total cosmic plan of God.[80] Thinking this way, Hegel believes, keeps one away from reflecting critically upon one's particular subjective appraisal of his or her freedom.

I think it is obvious that a predeterministic interpretation of history does not lend itself to the liberation of the oppressed; it is not geared toward the transformation of cultural forms. It legitimates the existence of social malfunctions in society as contributing to the ultimate plan of God.

If Afro-Americans had submitted themselves to the negative forces of history, based either on the belief that their social status was preordained or ordained by the natural forces of history, they would have perished in slavery. They made progress because they never accepted their social status as being the will of God. In fact, they argued that God's will is opposed to all notions of inferiorities and substandard conditions. A person or group should never feel that suffering caused by social malfunctions is the result of God's will. We must associate God's will with enhancing the quality of life for all persons, with the quest for social justice and equity among social groups. God's will is to be interpreted from the perspective of the self-actualization and self-fulfillment of all.

Hegel attempts to account for the problem of evil by suggesting that from the human side evil appears to be negative and pessimistic, but from the divine perspective it serves as a temporary means toward accomplishing an ultimate end. Consequently, because God's purpose always transcends the will of humans, from the human perspective the future might seem pessimistic, but from the divine perspective it is always optimistic.

Oppressed persons do not view their oppression as a necessary social evil used by God toward an ultimate end. We could never say that slavery was a necessary evil used by God to accomplish a goal, just as we find it inconceivable that God would use the persecution of Jews in Nazi Germany and blacks in South Africa toward an ultimate end. We must interpret God's purpose as opposing these inhuman forms of oppression.

Hegel and Black Africa

It is important to note that in his philosophy of history Hegel shared the nineteenth-century's prejudice against Africa and Afro-Americans. His philosophy of history is based on a comprehensive analysis of world history, which includes a discussion of the Oriental world, the Greek world, the Roman world, and the German world. In his rather brief discussion of the place of Africa in world history, his bias against black Africans becomes very apparent.

In the first instance, Hegel refuses to consider Africa as an integral part of world history. Africa, he says, "is no historical part of the World; it has no movement or development to exhibit."[81] The aspects of African civilization he considers to be a part of world history are associated with Asiatics and Europeans, not black Africans. "Historical movements in it — that is in its northern part — belong to the Asiatic or European World. . . . Egypt will be considered in reference to the passage of the human mind from its Western phase, but it does not belong to the African Spirit."[82] He considered black Africans an "Unhistorical, Undeveloped Spirit," whose orientation involved only the conditions of mere nature. Africa existed only on the threshold of the world's history.[83]

Because of his bias against the contribution of black Africans to world history, Hegel viewed the modern institution of slavery as an advancement for Afro-Americans.[84] Because black Africans did not contribute to the development of world history, Hegel considered them uncivilized. He believed that slavery was good for Afro-Americans because it took them from a state of mere isolated sensual existence.[85] After systematically negating the status of black Africans in Africa, Hegel asserted that slavery elevated black Africans to acquire education and to participate in a higher morality.[86]

Slavery is itself injustice, he continues, because the goal of humanity is toward freedom; but freedom is for the mature sectors of humanity. It is obvious that Hegel did not consider black Africans mature persons, because he failed to raise serious objections to their enslavement. After disregarding black Africans as integral to history and repudiating their sense of morality, Hegel endorsed their enslavement. "It is the essential principle of slavery, that man has not yet attained a consciousness of his freedom, and consequently sinks down to a mere Thing — an object of no value." He continued, "Among the Negroes moral sentiments are quite weak, or more strictly speaking, non-existent."[87]

Hegel's prejudice against the cultural contributions of black Africans represents a legacy that we have yet to overcome.[88] Cultural pluralism cannot exist in a society where discrimination exists. The nature of cultural pluralism requires peaceful coexistence among social groups. Because the cultural context of black Africans did not fit the conceptual framework of his metaphysical scheme, Hegel considered their cultural heritage to be of no value in world history. By willfully ignoring the great cultural heritage of ancient black Africa and silencing its authentic voices, Hegel imposed his narrow biases on Africans, which is a clear illustration of racism, provincialism, imperialism, and ethnocentrism.

When Hegel speaks about the essence of humanity and freedom developing through self-consciousness and characterizing the direction of history, it is clear that he did not consider black Africans as part of the process. What he does is abstract from the Eurocentric perspective normative criteria for defining the essence of humanity, and he then imposes those criteria on other cultures in the world. He abstracts from a closed nationalistic perspective and then universalizes its criteria for all of humanity.

Hegel believed that this was the type of truth philosophy sought to understand. Hegel argued that because God governs the world and because its events reflect God's preordained plan, only those things that have been developed as a result of God's plan "possess bona fide reality." It follows, therefore, that those aspects of existence, including the experience of Africans and Afro-Americans, that do not fit Hegel's particular comprehension of God's plan, are "negative, worthless existence."

The Significance of Alfred North Whitehead's Contributions in Interpreting Culture

The Various Models of Pluralism

Although there are many worthy metaphysical systems in Western philosophy and theology, very few construct a model of pluralism for interpreting culture as significant as Whitehead's. His resolution of the age-old dichotomy of reality's oneness and manyness has important implications for a pluralistic society. I am convinced that such a society needs to have a metaphysical construct that succeeds in clarifying the nature of pluralism ontologically. Whitehead achieves this. This achievement is even more significant when it is used to provide the framework for addressing the type of social justice issues basic to majority-minority relations.

A model of pluralism that does not advocate social justice for minority groups results in what I would call negative peaceful co-existence. This amounts to what can be described as the fallacy of misplaced cultural identity.

Whitehead's model of pluralism, by contrast, insists on the empowerment and intensification of each emerging possibility in the world. Thus, positive peaceful coexistence between majority and minority social groups, which is the foundation of cultural pluralism, is inherent in the Whiteheadian framework.

In a society characterized by inequity, it is difficult to develop a model of social pluralism that defines peaceful coexistence as ensuring social justice for all. Realizing this peaceful coexistence becomes problematic when one recognizes that American society emphasizes achievement, social mobility, and competition for all persons while at the same time constantly using sexism, racism, and other forms of discrimination against members of minority social groups.

We have seen that as early as the pre-Socratic tradition in philosophy the idea of pluralism was being advanced. Whitehead's significance, then, does not reside in originating the idea of pluralism in the West. His background in mathematics, physics, and philosophy, however, enabled him to reconstruct the idea of pluralism in a framework capable of overcoming the inadequacies of traditional approaches.

A Brief Look at Whitehead's Contribution

The first factor to be considered is the integrative approach Whitehead employs in philosophic method. Because we now live in an age of high technology and specialization, academic disciplines often tend to compartmentalize knowledge to the extent that we fail to understand its interrelatedness. Whitehead's philosophic method brings together insights from a variety of academic disciplines toward understanding modern culture. He integrates physics, religion, history, psychology, philosophy, and mathematics, among others. I would refer to his approach as a decompartmentalization of method. He frees modern culture from a fixation with narrowness and one-sidedness in methodology.

The complexity of the contemporary human condition requires us to take an integrative approach to the study of culture. No aspect of culture is isolated; each of its many features, from the simple to the complex, is interrelated. I will attempt to show later how this sense of interrelatedness can serve to safeguard against the problem of cultural normativeness discussed earlier. We will also see how Whitehead's ontological construct protects against using evaluative categories such as inferiority and superiority in describing different cultural experiences. True pluralism uses the principle of unity in diversity to characterize the nature of being. Whitehead's metaphysics succeeds at this point. He demonstrates this ontologically; we will draw out its implications for ethnic relations. These two factors — true pluralism and ethnic relations — should be integrated into a growing synthesis.

Why is this so urgent for American society? Because up until now pluralism has meant advantage for the majority and disadvantage for certain minorities, despite the nation's unparalleled diversity. The national motto of America is *E Pluribus Unum,* which means that from many different ethnic groups America has become one nation. When this motto was adopted in the eighteenth century, it primarily referred to the union of thirteen separate British colonies. Now, in the last quarter of the twentieth century, America has become to an even greater extent a nation of immigrants, with two notable exceptions.

The first exception is the full-blooded American Indians. Their forebears emigrated from Asia thousands of years before the English settlers arrived. Yet when we read American history, we get the impression that the discovery of America took place in 1492 with Columbus. A thorough account of American history would seem then to need to include the contributions made by Indians (as well as women, Afro-Americans, and other marginalized groups).[89]

The other exception is the Afro-American. Whereas other immigrants came to America voluntarily, Afro-Americans are the only ethnic minority social group that came to America by coercion. Afro-Americans came to America in chains and were forced into slavery.

America continues to become more ethnically diverse. "Since 1607, when the first permanent English settlers reached the New

World, at Jamestown, fully 44 million people have immigrated to what is now the United States." What we have in America is one of the largest immigration movements in world history.[90] If pluralism were based on ethnic structure alone, America would far exceed the standard. Such a social makeup makes the need for alternative models of pluralism urgent. Pluralism has positive implications for American society. But it should not have positive implications for some ethnic groups and negative implications for others. Pluralism has perpetuated and continues to perpetuate a polarization between majority and minority social groups, reducing many members of minority groups to marginality and boosting many members of the majority social group to the top of the socioeconomic ladder.

These inequities do not reflect the type of pluralism that can liberate the oppressed and the oppressor. Whitehead's model of pluralism, by contrast, points us in the direction of overcoming sexism, racism, and classism.

The integrative aspect of Whitehead's method can be seen more fully in the way he interprets experience. Using a comprehensive approach, his analysis includes both the inorganic and the organic. It interrelates nature and humanity. Humanity is not above the environment; the environment is not something for humanity to exploit. Humanity is a product of nature and an integral part of it. The critical task for modern humanity is to find and maintain an appropriate balance with nature. Whitehead's integrative approach helps to set the stage for this. It moves modern humanity in the direction of an ecological approach to culture.

Whitehead's idea of process or change is also basic to a new understanding of culture. Culture is not something self-contained and static. The tradition of substantialism, which was so important in Western philosophical heritage, is transformed in Whitehead's metaphysics into the realization of process and becoming as basic units of reality. The famous Heraclitean dictum "You never step in the same river twice," along with the ancient Greek philosopher Parmenides's notion that permanence is the basic unit of reality, are systematically integrated. In other words, permanence and change are not mutually exclusive. They are integrated components of one process. Each dimension of culture constantly experiences change. We witness this in our own time as oppressed minority groups demand and foster change and develop praxis-oriented theologies that reflect upon that change — black theologies, feminist theologies, a whole host of liberation theologies.

There is a radical element in process thought. It relates to change and becoming. "The pure conservative is fighting against the essence of the universe,"[91] says Whitehead. His point is that the very essence of the real is process. Each actual phenomenon in the world is to be understood only in light of its becoming and perishing. There is no halt to the process to the extent that the real is just its static self.

Change and becoming enable a civilization to understand what has been and what can be. Every culture must make a distinction between the two. It must possess the daring and vigor to move beyond the safeties of past accomplishments. In the face of change, however, lies the permanence and stability of the unchanging eternal objects.[92]

Another basic characteristic of culture is social relatedness. This brings into focus Whitehead's doctrine of social immanence, which will be dealt with later. It means that each existing thing in the world contains internal and external interrelatedness. Things are not individualized, separate, and detached from one another as in the Newtonian paradigm. It is Whitehead's notion of internal relatedness that makes genuine pluralism possible in his system. In his model we will see that he accounts for both individuality and corporeality while at the same time overcoming the inadequacies of dualism and monism.

Social relatedness opposes the idea of the majority social group projecting itself as the normative cultural pattern that dictates standards for minority social groups. The Whiteheadian notion makes self-realization primary, and that emphasis tends to lead toward an equitable distribution of power. The focus of Whitehead's vision is on "mutual cooperation"; it opposes the idea of the majority enforcing its will on the minority.[93]

Social relatedness emphasizes inclusiveness, not exclusiveness. Whitehead's model suggests that liberty, equality, and self-development are basic components of the nature of reality. But in order for this vision to become a reality in American society, we have to find a way of overcoming the exclusionary principle. By exclusionary principle I mean the centralization of decision-making processes in the majority social group. Afro-Americans and other oppressed minority social groups are not fully integrated into, and are usually in fact excluded from, the major decision-making structures — business firms, social institutions, and so forth.

Not only has this exclusionary principle affected majority-minority relations, but it fosters competition among ethnic minority groups. It militates against their ability to develop corporate strategies of liberation. It has erected barriers between social groups, cutting them off from one another.

Afro-Americans and Africans, for example, have yet to realize their commonality fully. We have also failed to see the common forms of oppression experienced by Afro-Americans and American Indians. Hispanics, an increasingly oppressed group in America and one of the fastest growing minorities in America, have not been able to ally their liberation efforts successfully with those of Afro-Americans. Each group feels that its liberation agenda is so unique that to unite efforts would minimize the impact. They fail to realize that true unity in diversity maximizes one's impact. Despite the fact that sexism and racism are products of white male domination, giving Afro-Americans and women a common basis of protest, they still find themselves competing in many instances rather than being mutually supportive.

Each oppressed group finds it difficult to affirm its unique identity and maintain a sense of individuality while at the same time cultivating an interdependent sense of corporate liberation. The power structure capitalizes on this disunity by manipulating these groups into internal strife over declining resources. It keeps them divided and fighting among themselves, which is a subtle way of maintaining control of all oppressed social groups, including poor whites.

The tragedy of poor whites is that they have been brainwashed by the power structure into accepting the notion of the cultural superiority of whites. They have accepted the belief that they are better than Afro-Americans primarily because of color. And likewise many Afro-Americans have been brainwashed into believing that they are inferior to whites because of color. Consequently, rather than uniting toward liberation around common goals, poor whites and Afro-Americans continue their antagonism, which keeps the powers and principalities of systemic oppression in control of both groups.

The Whiteheadian notion of "mutual cooperation" provides the context for overcoming this problem of cultural insulationism, which continually blocks the realization of genuine pluralism.

Whitehead's view of the self is yet another of his contributions toward interpreting culture. He succeeds in overcoming the Platonic and Cartesian tendency to bifurcate the self into two separate categories, mind and matter. Whitehead corrects this by suggesting that the self is an organism containing developmental processes. It is not static and complete; it is a nexus of emerging possibilities. The self is an enduring phenomenon in that it maintains identity through time. But this is not to say that it contains an underlying substance that endures change while remaining unchanged itself. That would represent the commonsense view of the self, which has characterized much of Western thought.

While the self maintains a sense of unity and identity, giving it a sense of stability and permanence, in reality the self is constantly changing. Its being is defined in the context of its becoming. It is a complex unity of events and experiences. None of these experiences within the self is detached and isolated, including mind and matter. As an interlocking nexus, mind and matter are two distinct manifestations of one process. They are socialized and integrated into a bundle of ongoing processes that affect each dimension of selfhood.

The significant insight here in Whitehead's view of the self is the notion of "relationality" as primary. The self as an organism coordinates millions of molecules within itself, making for a creative synthesis. This is to say that the self is more than a conglomerate of experiences. Rather, the self unifies a conglomerate of constantly emerging possibilities and synthesizes them into a sense of oneness.

This is why the idea of organism is more exemplary of the self than mechanism. Within a pluralistic society the goal is to discover ways of allowing self-actualization in the context of relationality. This requires an open system rather than a closed one. The Whiteheadian model is open. The self viewed as an organism is characterized by openness. Viewed as a mechanism it is characterized by closedness and invulnerability. For individuals in society to relate successfully to others they have to be open and vulnerable. And Whitehead's notion of interdependence, which is primary in his notion of the self, suggests that while maintaining a sense of openness to other ethnic social groups, one should also adhere to one's own unique ethnic tradition.

Finally, the idea of society in Whitehead's model has relevance for contemporary culture. A helpful way to describe it is by using a key insight from systems theory — namely, the recognition that society and the world in which we live consist of interrelated organisms. We can say that on the one hand the world itself consists of one large system. And on the other hand we can say that within that one large system is a multiplicity of sub-systems. That is, every dimension of reality is interrelated into a nexus of organisms.

It is apparent here that the idea of relationality is not only relevant for majority-minority intergroup relations, but it is also a basis for understanding everything in the world. As we continue to think through the implications of Whitehead's metaphysics for pluralism, the significance of relationality will become more apparent.

2

A Model for Cultural Pluralism: The Adequacy of Organic Pluralism in Process Metaphysics

Organic Pluralism:
A Shift in Metaphysical and Social Paradigms

The replacement of scientific materialism with the philosophy of organism represents a radical shift in paradigms. I believe that applying the principles of organic pluralism to majority-minority social groups in America can profoundly shift social paradigms. As I discuss the metaphysical dimensions of organic pluralism, I will suggest some ways in which they offer a radical modification for ethnicity in American society.

First of all, it will be helpful to clarify the basis of determining the adequacy of process metaphysics for accomplishing this goal. Therefore, I shall start by defining process metaphysics. In *Religion in the Making* Whitehead says, "By 'metaphysics' I mean the science which seeks to discover the general ideas which are indispensably relevant to the analysis of everything that happens."[1] The point here is that metaphysics, as used by Whitehead, concerns itself with both particular and universal aspects of experience. By "particular" Whitehead means that metaphysics begins with an analysis of human experience; then it makes broad generalizations about universal dimensions that characterize all acts of experience. This means that the adequacy of a metaphysical system is to be found in practice or experience itself.[2]

In this regard, the task of metaphysics is not solely to speculate about abstractions; rather, its task is to serve as a critic of the tendency in society to distort concrete acts of experience. These distortions occur through abstractions. Metaphysics seeks to describe reality without distorting it. In its descriptive analysis, metaphysics should be consistent with reality, and truth in metaphysics is found in such consistency. In other words, we should not modify reality to make it consistent with metaphysics. The effort of the philosopher/theologian should be always to revise metaphysical systems so as to make them more consistent with the reality being described. If inconsistency develops between the metaphysical scheme and the reality being described, the fault is to be found in the metaphysical scheme and not in practice. Whitehead says, "Whatever is found in 'practice' must lie within the scope of the metaphysical description. When the description fails to include the 'practice,' the metaphysics is inadequate and requires revision. There can be no appeal to practice to supplement metaphysics, so long as we remain contented with our metaphysical doctrines. Metaphysics is nothing but the description of generalities which apply to all details of practice."[3]

The way in which a society interprets the complex, dynamic processes involved in intergroup relations represents an example of abstracting cultural expressions from experience. How social groups perceive their identity in society always represents a growing tension between experience and abstraction. Any time persons reflect upon an aspect of experience in culture, they are engaging in various forms of abstraction. Talcott Parsons in *The Social System* refers to this when speaking about how cultural phenomena are analyzed. He says, "The general maxim that 'all observation is in terms of a conceptual scheme' applies to the observation of what we call cultural patterns just as much as to any other aspect of systems of action. It is a set of abstractions from the concrete phenomena of social action processes."⁴ The sexism, racism, classism, imperialism, provincialism, and ethnocentrism that militate against the peaceful coexistence of majority and minority social groups are examples of abstracting distortions from experience, distortions, moreover, that are detrimental to society. To develop a conceptual framework that seeks to overcome these social ills is the goal before us.

Tensions and Crisis in the Old Paradigm

We have seen how the problem of cultural normativeness, which developed in the materialist paradigm, represents a distortion of experience in that it elevates the culture of the majority social group as the standard for assimilation and amalgamation. In addition, its persistence in social structures stands contrary to cultural pluralism. Before we can appreciate fully how organic pluralism offers an alternative to this problem, we need to be keenly aware of the reasons why a paradigm shift in majority-minority intergroup relations is essential.

We can begin by saying that the old paradigm simply does not function in the interest of minority groups. It does not work for them. And, according to Thomas S. Kuhn, one of the primary indications of the need for a paradigm shift is the dysfunctionality of the old paradigm.⁵ For example, in 1926 Robert E. Park, a leading social scientist whose theories on race relations reflect the old social paradigm, developed the theory of a race relations cycle, a theory describing the assimilation process characteristic of all ethnic minorities in America. As we saw in the previous chapter, the race relations cycle, as Park describes it, starts when minority groups make contact with the majority social group; they then engage in competition and accommodation and inevitably become assimilated into the dominant culture.⁶ All minority groups, Park assumes, experience this.

The inadequacy of Park's theory is that its monocultural orientation fails to take account of the pervasive sexism, racism, and classism that have prevented oppressed minority groups such as women, Afro-Americans, American Indians, and Mexican Americans from competing in American society. Not only does the new paradigm require us to show more sensitivity to the unique circumstances of these oppressed social groups, but it also seeks creative ways of eradicating the circumstances that produce marginal existence.

Although Gunnar Myrdal's *magnum opus, An American Dilemma*, published in 1944, criticized the *laissez-faire* attitude of social scientists in regard to ethnic minority social groups, he assumed that "it is to the advantage of American Negroes as individuals and as a group to become assimilated into American culture, to acquire the traits held in esteem by the dominant white Americans."[7] It is true that Myrdal's position is exemplary of liberal assimilationism. But it becomes even more problematic when used as a model for cultural pluralism because it perpetuates the majority social group's cultural normativeness. The result exalts the ideal of unity in conformity that is characteristic of monocultural assimilation. By contrast, the new paradigm upholds the principle of unity in diversity. As I will attempt to show later, such a model requires a multicultural approach, one that is capable of overcoming cultural normativeness.

In sum, although early studies in cultural assimilation in the American society have always shifted between extreme closed nationalism on the one hand and a form of liberal assimilationism on the other hand, the notion of cultural normativeness has persisted, and couched under the rubric of "the melting pot theory," it has functioned contrary to a pluralistic model. While it is true that the melting pot theory began to experience a significant decline in 1963 upon the publication of the award-winning volume *Beyond the Melting Pot* by Nathan Glazer and Daniel Patrick Moynihan, in reality cultural normativeness continues to prevail. There is an urgent need to undergird the new paradigm with a radically different conceptual framework.

The effort to shift from one paradigm to another always involves a crisis.[8] But in spite of the inevitability of the crisis, the urgency of the matter makes it imperative that we abandon the old closed materialist paradigm, which fosters cultural normativeness, in favor of the new organic paradigm, based on social relatedness and relativity. But why is a crisis inevitable whenever persons attempt to make a paradigm shift? Talcott Parsons helps us to understand why in his discussion of "Institutionalized Rationalization" and "Cultural Lag." He mentions three types of repercussions resulting from institutional change.

The first repercussion he describes as "the restructuring of occupational roles themselves." Based on new knowledge, new occupational roles are created and old roles are redefined. "For example in the scientific field, only in fairly recent years did such a thing as a 'nuclear physicist' exist. William Welch was the first professional 'pathologist' in the history of American medicine, and only about the turn of the last century did the role of 'sociologist' emerge."[9]

Social analysts observe that in a pluralist society dominated by a majority social group, minority social groups remain in a subordinate role. The new paradigm calls for a radical modification of occupational roles that minority persons have traditionally held. In the past, for example, women have been relegated to occupational roles subordinate to men. American society accepted this as normative. We can see this reflected in all aspects of society. But the feminist movement now is calling for equality of opportunity for women. The masses of Afro-Americans, too, have always been consigned to menial jobs, despite their protestations against subordinate occupational roles and demands for justice and equality.

Affirmative action programs to assist minority groups in job placement have not reached most members of each group. Most remain in subordinate roles. For example, American corporations continue to be controlled almost exclusively by white males. The same pattern persists in other sectors. Some businesses and social organizations are trying to overcome this by establishing quota systems designed to recruit minority persons and place them in responsible positions. In settings where additional training is needed, the minority persons are given opportunities to acquire the technical skills needed for the job. This means that some positions in companies that would have traditionally been channeled to white males are now being earmarked for minority persons. Such a process represents the beginning of a significant paradigm shift. The racial imbalance in the work force will not correct itself automatically. It requires an earnest commitment on the part of those in power to redress the legacy of inequality.

Parsons emphasizes that further repercussions result from this type of change because persons in control of existing resources in social institutions have a vested interest in maintaining their ways of doing things, maintaining their status, and receiving remuneration. Therefore the incumbents of occupational roles that are superseded usually become threatened by the advancement of minority persons and thus become defensive. We can observe such a pattern in churches, schools, public service institutions, federal agencies, and businesses.

The second type of repercussion Parsons notes has to do with changing the character and structure of the organization. Social institutions, it seems to me, should model a pluralistic society, striving to be exemplary of ethnic diversity in every respect. In other words, it is not enough for social institutions controlled by majority social groups to employ a few minority persons and feel that they have attained pluralism. In order to break down the economic barriers between majority and minority groups, social institutions must begin to employ minority persons in large numbers.

The third repercussion relates to power. Members of the majority social group are often reluctant to share power with members of minority groups. In the old paradigm the majority social group maintained a monopoly on the control of resources. But the new paradigm requires an equitable distribution of resources. Minority persons want to participate in making the decisions that affect their lives. They want to become more active in institutional governance and control.

The present generation is no longer interested in whether the presuppositions and beliefs of the new paradigm are true. It is already committed to discovering the paradigm's implications for reorienting majority-minority relations.

Experience and the New Paradigm

The basis for the metaphysic of organic pluralism is found in Whitehead's interpretation of experience. The phrase Whitehead uses to describe experience is "actual entity" (at times he uses "actual occasion"). Actual entities, he contends, "are the final things of which the world is made up."[10] We cannot go behind actual entities to find anything more real.[11] They are final reality. The new paradigm replaces irreducible bits of matter, as the final acts of experience, with quanta of energy. The irreducible bits of matter, which were the fountainhead of the Newtonian materialist cosmology, are now transformed into microphysical energy systems, such as protons and electrons. Whitehead calls actual entities "drops of experience."[12] The totality of reality, including persons, is made of these expressions of experience.

These expressions of experience are complex and dynamic organisms. They are not static and substantial, as they were conceived in scientific materialism. Whitehead abandons the notion that the final acts of experience consist of substances undergoing change while remaining in substance unchanged.

In Whitehead's organic pluralism what guards against any experience of culture asserting itself as normative over against others, as in cultural normativeness, is the fact that all experiences are equal ontologically.[13] They are made of the same stuff. Although experiences differ among themselves, they all bear the same ontological status. "The final facts are, all alike, actual entities."[14] Not only are there differences in experiences, but there are also gradations of experiences. These differences, however, do not make any instance of experience ontologically superior or inferior to any other. They are ontologically the same.

In this discussion I am using the word *ontological* interchangeably with *metaphysical*. Both words attempt to describe the nature of reality. Specifically, they are concerned with the being of final reality. In this regard, we can say that in process metaphysics the being of all instances of experience contains ontological equality. Whitehead points out that "the generic character of an actual entity should include God as well as the lowest actual occasion, though there is a specific difference between the nature of God and that of any occasion."[15] The difference Whitehead is referring to here is not a generic distinction between God and other actual entities. Indeed, one of his major concerns in developing a natural theology is to avoid such distinctions. The nature of God does not differ from other actual entities in generic quality; rather, God differs in function.

Consequently, if we extrapolate from Whitehead's approach to experience and apply it to social structures, we discover that in the new paradigm the basis for intergroup relations becomes one of relativity and social relatedness. Rather than allowing the majority social group to project itself as the norm for the acculturation and assimilation of minority groups, a Whiteheadian approach would suggest mutuality and interdependence as the appropriate characteristics for culture formation.

Organic pluralism also disallows projecting any one experience as normative for culture formation when it declares that the final facts of experience are not extended substances, as in both the Aristotelian and Newtonian cosmologies. Whenever the real is perceived as solely permanent, static, absolute, and unchanging, people tend to elevate it over against other experiences that appear to be different. By contrast, Whitehead helps us to realize that the final facts of experience are not self-contained, separate, independent, and unchanging. Because the being of each actual entity is dependent upon the being of other experiences, each instance of experience has to become vulnerable to the other. The emphasis, therefore, is on each experience attaining its highest possibilities.

When we view tangible objects — tables, desks, chairs, pencils, stones — the commonsense interpretation, which has been present in Western philosophical thought since Aristotle's doctrine of substance, holds these objects as concrete. In reality they are cultural abstractions from the concrete. Whitehead refers to tangible objects, which appear to be self-enduring, as a society of actual occasions.[16]

Although physical objects appear to consist of sameness, permanence, and stability, in reality the energy systems they are composed of are changing constantly. Therefore, the way we describe things in the world consists of abstractions from experiences of processes or systems. The concrete consists of creative processes that microphysical particles undergo as they constantly change from potentiality to actuality. Each actual entity contains individuality, which is manifested in its self-actualization. Whitehead does not dissolve individuality into a form of monism; in other words, reality does not consist of homogeneous collectivity. Rather, each actual entity has value and significance of itself. It possesses self-identity, self-determination, self-creativity, and self-diversity. Each actual entity is a creative synthesis of many possibilities merging into a single whole. At the point of its own "concrescence," which identifies the process of completion, each actual entity experiences intensification and satisfaction. The real individuality of each actual entity is crucial in that one cannot have a metaphysic of genuine pluralism without a theory of individuality.

Moreover, important to each actual entity is social transcendence and novelty. Each experiences a sense of exclusiveness on the one hand, and inclusiveness on the other. Its exclusiveness is depicted in its inherent uniqueness, independence, difference, and the new contribution it makes to the whole. In this manner it transcends all other actual entities; or, to put it another way, it goes beyond them. Its inclusiveness refers to its social immanence, social relatedness, and organic interdependence. Whitehead refers to the exclusiveness, which is peculiar to everything in the world, when he says, "An actual occasion is a novel entity diverse from any entity in the many which it unifies."[17] And when he says reality is interconnected at every dimension of existence, he is referring to the inclusiveness of each phenomenon. Whitehead succeeds in allowing for both. "The creative process is a process of exclusion to the same extent as it is a process of inclusion."[18]

Process

Process describes the becoming of events. Process itself takes place within the creative advance of the world. And *creativity* names the universal metaphysical condition of all events in process. White-head says, "Creativity is the universal of universals characterizing ultimate matter of fact."[19] Therefore, all events that reach self-actualization undergo creativity. All phenomena are in the process of becoming, and the process is the becoming of events. Creativity is the ultimate principle that process employs in the becoming of actual occasions. Creativity is not substantial. In fact, as a category of the ultimate, creativity replaces Aristotle's category of primary substance.

Whitehead views creativity, the one, and the many as ultimate metaphysical principles. "The one" describes the singularity and individuality of each actual occasion. The one, therefore, is presupposed by the many, and the category of the many is presupposed by the one. The term *many* depicts the disjunctive, diversified aspect of actual occasions, which are always a conglomeration. The growing creative synthesis, which is characteristic of each actual occasion, is the process unifying disjunctive actual occasions into conjunctive-ness. Then creativity is the principle "by which the many, which are the universe disjunctively, become the one actual occasion, which is the universe conjunctively. It lies in the nature of things that the many enter into complex unity."[20]

Not only does Whitehead use the categories of actual entities or occasions to describe things in nature and the environment; he also uses them to describe persons. For example, like everything else, persons consist in actual entities. Whitehead is careful to avoid making any ontological bifurcations between persons and other things in the world; they are all made of the same basic stuff. This understanding does not mean, however, that persons cease to have uniqueness and significance. Their uniqueness resides in what can be referred to as self-awareness, that is, our awareness of our own awareness. It is the same as reflective consciousness. Not only does the human species know that it knows, but it demonstrates this by attaining such high levels of growth and development in all areas of life. This is unlike other species. One is not to infer from this that other species do not possess consciousness. It means that the consciousness manifested in the human species is more complex and configured.

Also important in Whitehead's view of persons is his integration of the spiritual and the physical. Both the soul and the body consist of actual entities or occasions. In this sense, the phrase "society of actual occasions" is appropriate to describe what a person is. The soul consists of a society of actual occasions, as does the body. Thus, even though the soul is singular and the body is singular, each consists of a multiplicity of events, happenings, and experiences. The body and soul are socialized, rather than individualized. They function as integrative, interwoven, interlocking networks of one and the same process. Here Whitehead captures a vision of the self as a psycho-physical unity. It is not bifurcated. It is holistic and inclusive. Unlike the mechanistic view of the self found in the supernaturalist tradition, which separates body from soul and creates a chasm between spirituality and social transformation, Whitehead's perspective maintains an appropriate balance.

The self for Whitehead does not consist of closed substances. The self is not complete; nor is it fixed. It represents a continued process of becoming. Like everything else in the world, persons are manifestations of emerging possibilities, continually being born and perishing.

Social Implications

Now, since creativity resides at the base of all cultural expressions, it becomes the task of social institutions to facilitate the realization of the essential values present in each social group. Because creativity, as a metaphysical category, inherently is neither positive nor negative, it is the task of the institutionalization process to bring out the positive possibilities contained in each social group as it seeks to make a contribution to the creative advance of the world. Such cultural forms as customs, mores, and traditions are managed through social institutions. The quality of management and leadership executed in social institutions in large measure determines the extent to which we enhance or impede the creative advance of the world.

For social groups to achieve self-fulfillment, each has to possess a certain degree of power and independence. Without a sense of self-worth, self-identity, and self-determination, which is the basis of independence, no social group can attain fulfillment. This is to say, each social group should maintain its own unique cultural features through aesthetics, language, customs, mores, art forms, and history. No social group can make a contribution to society without its adherents possessing strong independence. Whitehead is correct in pointing out that the essence of self-fulfillment is definiteness. Definiteness means individuality and independence. The absence of definiteness and individuality within a social group leads to discontent, rage, and militant responses on the part of its members.

For example, during the 1960s when the champion of the civil rights struggle, Martin Luther King, Jr., successfully led America into the integration of public accommodations, Afro-Americans were initially elated. But later the enthusiasm descended into bitter discontent, rage, and militancy; Afro-Americans realized that they still did not possess a sense of socioeconomic independence. The way we continue to interpret and practice social integration abets cultural and economic dependency on the part of Afro-Americans and other oppressed minority social groups. By this I mean that the continued presence of cultural normativeness in America constrains Afro-Americans and other minorities to emulate the economic structure and the culture of the majority if they want to be accepted, while at the same time they are forced to endure discrimination. When, after the civil rights movement, the majority social group refused to share power and control of resources equitably, Afro-Americans responded with disaffection and anger. This is what gave rise to the black power movement in the 1960s. The major quest for Afro-Americans was for independence.

This quest for independence does not mean that Afro-Americans want to exist separately and in isolation from other social groups. Their primary aspiration is to coexist peacefully alongside other social groups. But coexistence presupposes the presence of both independence and interdependence among all participating social groups.

I believe that Afro-Americans, women, American Indians, Africans, Latin Americans, Mexican Americans, and others have long recognized the very insight that is being expressed in process metaphysics, namely, that at the core of all occasions of experience resides an interconnectedness, because reality is from beginning to end integrated into togetherness. The majority social group, however, in attempting to monopolize resources, has prevented this truth from being realized in society on a large scale.

It is important to note that this togetherness does not destroy the uniqueness inherent within each emerging act of experience. Rather, when togetherness contains both independence and interdependence, it enriches the uniqueness of each participating social group. Creative union heightens independence and interdependence. It does not destroy them. The tragedy of the majority's idea of "integration" is its deliberate attempt to destroy the cultural uniqueness of minority social groups through asserting a monocultural ethos as the normative criterion of acculturation and assimilation.

Cultural Relativity:
From Unity in Conformity to Unity in Diversity

Throughout this chapter I will continue discussing the cultural factors involved in making a paradigm shift. After establishing Whitehead's metaphysical basis for relativity as a universal principle, I will then attempt to show its implications for cultural pluralism.

Relativity as a Universal Principle

Whitehead describes relativity as follows:

> That the potentiality for being an element in a real concrescence of many entities into one actuality is the one general metaphysical character attaching all entities, actual and non-actual; and that every item in its universe is involved in each concrescence. In other words, it belongs to the nature of a "being" that it is a potential for every "becoming." This is the "principle of relativity."[21]

In the old Newtonian paradigm reality was perceived as complete and actual. Consequently, reality did not contain relationality, which is essential for relativity. Because reality was thought to be self-contained and autonomous, the world did not possess any movement from potentiality to actuality.

The materialist approach to the world did not end with the death of Newton; its persistence in the physical sciences prevailed in modern science. Thomas Kuhn reminds us that "most physical scientists assumed that the universe was composed of microscopic corpuscles and that all natural phenomena could be explained in terms of corpuscular shape, size, motion and interaction. The nest of commitments proved to be both metaphysical and methodological."[22] Milic Capek makes the acute observation that the present generation continues many remnants of Newtonian science. Capek argues that the persistence of our Newtonian habits of viewing the world is merely reflective of deep, underlying mental habits: "We are all unconsciously Newtonians . . . and the classical idea of world-wide instants, containing simultaneous spatially separated events, still haunts the subconscious even of relativistic physicists."[23]

Whitehead displaces this static notion of reality and replaces it with the idea that every occasion has potential for entering into the becoming of other actual occasions. In other words, Whitehead universalizes the principle that every existing experience has the possibility of having an impact on the past and future of every other existing experience. And each occasion is internally related to every other experience. Nothing in the world exists in isolation. Whitehead says, "My theory involves the entire abandonment of the notion that simple location is the primary way in which things are involved in space-time. In a certain sense, everything is everywhere at all times. For every location involves an aspect of itself in every other location. Thus every spatio-temporal standpoint mirrors the world."[24]

Based on quantum theory, which is the direct antithesis of the old paradigm, organic relationality characterizes all existence. Whatever happens to any aspect of reality, regardless of how infinitesimal or complex, has implications for the totality of reality. The fact that each thing in the world is related both internally and externally to every other thing means that nothing is conceived in a vacuum or exists in isolation. Whitehead makes it clear that one cannot abstract the universe from any existing thing, actual or nonactual, so as to think of it in total isolation. "Whenever we think of some entity, we are asking, what is it fit for here? In a sense, every entity pervades the whole world."[25] This means that relationality presupposes relativity. Whereas the idea of democracy in America is built upon the premise that each person has the right to be different and to maintain a degree of self-determination, which is a primary characteristic of the philosophy of unity in diversity, every effort has been made by the American society, either by compulsion or persuasion, to protect the cultural dominance of the majority social group and to mold ethnic minority social groups into conformity with it. Consequently, when we develop social theories, social philosophies, legislation, and social policy outlining the principles of unity in diversity as it relates to ethnic pluralism, we inevitably tend to describe unity in conformity; the culture prescribed by the majority social group is always presupposed as normative.

The Need for Re-education

Philosopher John Dewey, addressing the National Education Association in 1916, was appropriately critical of this tendency to practice the philosophy of unity in conformity in the name of the democratic way of life, at the expense of devising creative ways to help minority social groups maintain a sense of ethnic consciousness.

Dewey pointed out that we should exercise caution in the way we use such designations as Irish American, German American, and so on because we assume "something which is already in existence called America, to which the other factors may be externally hitched on."[26] In reality the typical American is international and interracial in composition, and there is a significant danger in subsuming one's ethnic consciousness (whether that consciousness be Irish, German, African, Mexican, or whatever) beneath one's "Americanness." There is danger in separating each ethnic group in America from its particular history and cultural expression.

It is apparent that Afro-Americans, women, and other minority social groups need to discover their own "true consciousness" through the process of self-determination. One place in which this makes a significant difference is in our philosophies of education. For example, if one embraces the principle of unity in diversity as integral to the educational process, then one should support the notion that the whole educational approach, beginning with early grade school and extending through graduate school, should integrate into the curriculum the vast cultural contributions of those ethnic minority groups that helped to shape our composite society. Such an approach needs to be executed with intentionality, and should be integrated into religious education as well. Dewey anticipated this need. He said, "I wish our teaching of American history in the schools would take more account of the great waves of migration by which our land for over three centuries has been continuously built-up and make every pupil conscious of the rich breadth of our national make-up."[27]

Books written by social scientists and historians about American history rarely include the contributions of Afro-Americans, women, and American Indians, for instance, in a significant way. Those ethnic minorities which do not fit into the normative cultural paradigm are not integrated fully in American history. This indicates that our philosophies of education in America are geared toward the principle of unity in diversity only in theory, not in practice. In practice we tend to embrace the principle of unity in conformity.

The conformity approach is present not only in the way in which we deal with history; it invades other academic disciplines as well. But if we would employ the principle of unity in diversity in our philosophies of education, it would help us discover the ways in which each academic discipline could facilitate pluralism in both methodology and content. Diversity is an asset to an academic discipline, not a liability.

It is important, on the one hand, to continue offering a variety of ethnic studies in academic institutions. It affirms the fact that America is a heterogeneous society. It is far from being a melting pot. For this reason courses that deal with Afro-American studies, feminist studies, American Indian studies, Asian American studies, Latin American studies, and so forth serve a very vital function. But, on the other hand, the way in which we tend to include such course offerings in the curriculum fails to integrate them fully into the larger body of knowledge; we merely compartmentalize them and treat them as sub-units to the basic curriculum, rather than making them an integral part of the basic curriculum.

The shift from a monocultural orientation in studying ethnicity in America to a multicultural approach must begin by uprooting the fundamental cultural ethos that sustains social polarization between majority and minority social groups; it must begin, in short, by uprooting the phenomenon of cultural normativeness.

Talcott Parsons helps us to understand that cultural norms refer to social patterns, symbols, and beliefs that groups use as objects of orientation, action, communication, identification, and interaction. Cultural norms usually become integrated into the fabric of society, always resulting in institutionalization.[28] Because our traditional approach to majority-minority relations was centralized and based on the majority social group's norm, and because the nature of institutional change is gradual and reactionary, it is not surprising that some people resist abandoning the old paradigm. Martin Luther King, Jr., alluded to this when he said:

America has brought the nation and the world to an awe inspiring threshold of the future. Through our scientific and technological genius we have built mighty bridges to span the seas and skyscraping buildings to kiss the skies. We have dwarfed distance and placed time in chains. We have carved highways through the stratosphere. Through the marvelous advances of medical science we have been able to cure many dread plagues and diseases, alleviate our pain, prolong our lives, and make for greater security and physical well-being. This is a dazzling picture of America's scientific progress.

But when we turn to the question of progress in the area of race relations, we face one of the most shameful chapters of the American scene. In spite of the jet-like pace of our scientific and technological development, we still creep at horse and buggy speed in human relations.[29]

When students, faculties, and the general public learn to recognize the diversity that has shaped America, each ethnic group will then have the opportunity to appreciate its particular heritage, while at the same time appreciating more fully the rich contributions of the whole. Dewey put it this way: "In short, unless our education is nationalized in a way which recognizes that the peculiarity of our nationalism is its internationalism, we shall breed enmity and division in our frantic efforts to secure unity."[30] Only in this way can we begin to overcome our fixation with unity in conformity and start embracing the principle of unity in diversity.

America is not a melting pot. The old social paradigm that encouraged the melting pot concept in race relations goes against cultural relativity. It also goes against self-identity and self-determination, which are essential aspects of cultural pluralism. Among the many social ills bred by the melting pot theory as the traditional approach to integration is the control of resources by the majority social group. In such a system minority social groups have no basic control of their existential situation. They merely become assimilated into a cultural context that dissolves their uniqueness. As I pointed out earlier, this happens with many white ethnic groups, and as a result they usually move up the socioeconomic ladder. But for Afro-Americans this is made impossible because of the barriers posed by the color-line.

We have made color so pivotal in determining sociocultural acceptance that in stratification and social mobility America begins to resemble a caste system. In other words, the sociocultural context of social institutions in America suggests that being born white is positive, and being born nonwhite is negative. The principle of unity in diversity repudiates this imbalance and seeks fully to embrace multiethnic distinctions and thus avoid racism, sexism, ethnocentrism, and provincialism. This is what cultural relativity implies.

This radical shift to a new social paradigm would liberate the white social group from its tendency to perpetuate cultural normativeness throughout the global village. It would also liberate oppressed minority groups from a state of marginal existence. Such an approach would allow social groups in America to exemplify mutuality, inclusiveness, relativity, and social relatedness. This new shift calls for a revolution in the sociocultural context of majority-minority intergroup relations. It causes us to see social groups differently. It opposes both overt and covert forms of racism and sexism. Thomas Kuhn describes the shift in paradigms as elementary prototypes transformed, and he says that this can be illustrated by a switch in visual gestalt. "What were ducks in the scientist's world before the revolution are rabbits afterwards. The [person] who first saw the exterior of the box from above later sees its interior from below."[31] Whereas Thomas Kuhn speaks of these changes in reference to the scientific community, my effort is to pose them to the social, behavioral, and humanistic sciences, as well as to society in general. Radical change takes place frequently among elite scientists, but we must find ways to effect the shift for the laity. It is only when the new paradigm becomes integrated into life-style that the "switch in visual gestalt" makes a significant difference in society. The maturation of movements to eradicate sexism, racism, prejudice, and discrimination is an indicator of the emergence of this switch in visual gestalt.

Thomas Kuhn recognizes that changes in scientific paradigms always take time. Because of this, concomitant with the paradigm shift is the need for training. He uses the following example to illustrate this point.

> Looking at a contour map, the student sees lines on paper, the cartographer a picture of a terrain. Looking at a bubble-chamber photograph, the student sees confused and broken lines, the physicist a record of familiar subnuclear events. Only after a number of such transformations of vision does the student become an inhabitant of the scientist's world, seeing what the scientist sees and responding as the scientist does. The world that the student then enters is not, however, fixed once and for all by the nature of the environment, on the one hand, and of science, on the other. Rather, it is determined jointly by the environment and the particular normal-scientific tradition that the student has been trained to pursue.[32]

The shift in social paradigms necessitates an ongoing re-education process that promotes cultural relativity, one that is able to influence every segment of society. Such a process combines thought and action. It displaces all paternalistic attitudes peculiar to the old paradigm and begins to integrate the principle of social relatedness and interdependence. This re-education cannot be relegated solely to the laboratory of the scientist or to the classrooms of academic institutions; it has to become the guiding cultural ethos of our modern consciousness.

From the Hierarchical Model to the Ecological Perspective

After examining some of the damage that adherence to the hierarchical model has done to nature and to majority-minority relations, we will then be prepared to appreciate more fully the importance of adopting an ecological perspective. It will become apparent in this discussion that Whitehead's organic pluralism is compatible with the ecological approach.

The Hierarchical Model

The philosophical and theological background of the hierarchical model grew out of an integration of Aristotle's philosophy of substance and the biblical tradition of Judeo-Christianity. It is important to note that not only did Aristotle's metaphysics prevail as the basis of truth in ancient Greece, but his system of thought served as the foundation of metaphysical speculation in the West up until the decline of medievalism in the modern period. Whitehead remarked that Aristotle was one of the chief metaphysicians in all of Western history. Aristotle's great achievement in correcting Plato's dichotomy of matter and spirit, the Christianization of his metaphysics into Thomism during the medieval period, his theological anthropology, doctrine of God, metaphysics, and political philosophy — all these attest to the magnitude of Aristotle's contributions to the development of Western philosophy and theology.

But Aristotle's philosophy of substance ushered into Western thought the subject-object mode of thinking manifested in a hierarchical approach to the world, which becomes quite problematic for majority-minority intergroup relations. Since the subject-object approach will be dealt with later, let us now concentrate on some social ill effects of the hierarchical model, before showing how the ecological perspective provides an alternative.

Aristotle contended that the world consists of a hierarchy of substances. The substances contain different degrees of importance, meaning that some levels of existence are believed to be superior to others. For example, at the bottom of the scale of the hierarchy of substances are such elements as earth, water, air, and fire. The next level consists of plants and animals; humanity stands above this level, and God is at the top of the hierarchy.[33] Some of the underlying implications of the hierarchical model that have proved to have devastating consequences in the modern period are dominance, exploitation, competition, instrumentality, and utility.

Modern humanity used the biblical tradition to substantiate the idea of dominance and subordination. Frequently quoted passages in this regard are Genesis 1:26 and Psalm 8:3–6:

> And God said, Let us make man in our image, after our likeness: and let them have dominion over the fish of the sea, and over the fowl of the air, and over the cattle, and over all the earth, and over every creeping thing that creepeth upon the earth.

> When I consider thy heavens, the work of thy fingers, the moon and the stars, which thou hast ordained; What is man that thou art mindful of him? and the son of man, that thou visitest him? For thou hast made him a little lower than the angels, and hast crowned him with glory and honour.[34]

During the formation of the modern period we used these and other passages of Scripture to justify the exploitation of nature and the depersonalization of Afro-Americans, women, and American Indians, as I will illustrate.

It is important to note, on the one hand, as Sir William Cecil Dampier points out in his important volume, *History of Science*, that ancient Greece, the Renaissance, and the twentieth century represent the three periods in the history of humankind in which our most advanced intellectual contributions are found. These have been times when nations were expanding both geographically and economically. And the crowning feature in each period was the quest for increased economic stability and opportunities for the leisured life.[35] But, on the other hand, we need to be aware that America and other European nations achieved a leisured life in large measure by raping Africa of its wealth, territory, and human and natural resources.[36] The American institution of slavery created a social ill unlike any other experience of slavery in human history. John Hope Franklin points out that the institution of slavery was widespread during the earliest known history of many developing peoples, including Africans, Greeks, and Romans.[37] But, according to W. E. B. Du Bois, it was only during the modern institution of slavery that slavery became associated almost exclusively with blackness.[38] The hierarchical model, as practiced presently, still consigns the masses of Afro-Americans to subordinate roles in society, where they continue to struggle toward attaining a viable social status.[39]

It is true that the scientific discoveries of the modern period inevitably enhanced the quality of life. But alongside these technological achievements and the advances in scientific experimentation came social problems that continue to plague the present generation.

Whereas the medieval period was characterized by religious authoritarianism, supernaturalism, and Aristotle's speculative metaphysics, which became manifested in the systematic theology of Saint Thomas Aquinas, the birth of the modern period was characterized by thoroughgoing individualism, nationalism, and scientific experimentation and observation. In the modern period the church ceased to be the predominant social force in society.

It was during this period of increasing knowledge, expansion, and quest for wealth that notions of competition, dominance, individualism, exploitation, instrumentality,[40] and utility[41] became institutionalized in the hierarchical model. What brought this to fruition was the fact that in the early development of America and during its attempt to compete with developing European powers, the exploitation of nature and the depersonalization of Afro-Americans and American Indians were encouraged.

The competitive struggle was facilitated by the Commercial Revolution. It fostered the revitalization of the European economy, the decline of feudalism, the creation of towns, an increasing interest in commercial activities, and the recognition that the acquisition of wealth brought about power and leisure. The competition created was characterized by ruthless exploitation of both human and environmental resources. The emergence of strong nations in Western Europe provided channels for this competition. These states encouraged their citizens to employ any effective means of competitive trading.[42] John Hope Franklin describes this type of competitiveness in the following manner:

> The birth of the modern period gave to humanity a new sense of freedom. This new found freedom was defined on the basis of what would benefit the individual. The quest for it was pursued by individuals with such passion that it resulted in the eradication of long established principles and beliefs, such as adherence to infallibility and external authority. Individuals began assuming responsibility for themselves. Also, in this search for freedom came the destruction of the rights of others to pursue the same ends for their gain.[43]

Because the hierarchical model placed humanity on a stratum higher than plants and "lower" animals, modern humanity felt justified in its exploitation of nature; and because that model placed white males above all other human beings, those white males felt justified in exploiting women and nonwhite males. They believed they were doing God's will in their conquest of natural and human resources. Knowledge was used as a means of achieving mastery and dominance. The majority social group tried to become the master and possessor of natural and human resources.[44]

The hierarchical model, when manifested through the extreme individualism and competitiveness of the modern period, gave sanction to the emasculation of the black male, forced the black woman to assume primary leadership of the black family structure, dehumanized American Indians, and consigned white and black women to subordinate occupational roles.

The extreme individualism so characteristic of the modern period did not decline with the emergence of evolutionary theory in the nineteenth and early twentieth century; individualism was merely reformulated into an evolutionary perspective. After the publication of Charles Darwin's epoch-making *The Origin of Species* in 1859, theoreticians throughout the West seized upon it as a breakthrough and began immediately to apply the evolutionary theory to their respective disciplines. Sociologists, anthropologists, theologians, historians, economists, psychologists, and political scientists pondered the meaning of Darwinism for society.[45]

In its social form, Darwinism was used to legitimize racism, sexism, and imperialism. In the natural order, where competition and the fight for territory reigned among lower animals, the fittest were perceived to be those species possessing the power, dominance, and ability to control the weaker species. Social Darwinists then extrapolated this to the human arena and argued that inequitable distribution of resources and imbalances of power among races were the way things ought to be. From this emerged a philosophy of militarism designed to keep the weaker races subordinate. This philosophy suggested that social inequities and injustice are basic consequences of the natural evolutionary process.[46]

Prior to the 1890s social Darwinism took the form of rugged individualism. From this came the ruthless business competition and the exploitive economics and politics that America justified as survival philosophy. The races that did not have the resources to compete were considered weaker and unfit.

Darwinian individualism later was shaped into a philosophy of international expansion and conquest. European powers and American society adapted the survival-of-the-fittest motif to international conflict ideologies.[47]

It is true that the social Darwinism of the late nineteenth and early twentieth century has declined in popularity; but the survival-of-the-fittest motif became so ingrained into our modern consciousness that shades of it persist in different forms even today.

The Ecological Alternative

Clearly the hierarchical model in its traditional form is contrary to cultural pluralism. Let us now turn our attention to the ecological perspective to see how it offers an alternative to the problems created by the hierarchical model.

The ecological perspective represents a significant development of the organic approach. It is unique in that it applies the principle of interrelatedness in investigating the relation organisms have to their environment. The philosophy of organism developed in process metaphysics is quite compatible with the study of environmental and human ecology. Although Whitehead uses the word *organism* infrequently, it is apparent that from start to finish his metaphysical scheme is organic. Whitehead ascribes two meanings to organism. The microscopic meaning refers to the formal constitution of an actual occasion. And the macroscopic meaning "is concerned with the givenness of the actual world, considered as the stubborn fact which at once limits and provides opportunity for the actual occasion."[48]

The point of departure in the organic perspective is quite different from that in the hierarchical perspective. The hierarchical model is based on the concept of an individualized context, meaning that each unit of reality is perceived as self-contained. In fact, the term *hierarchy* is derived from the Greek words *hieros*, "sacred," and *archos*, "ruler."[49] By contrast, the context of the ecological perspective is socialized, meaning that things are interdependent.

Although there are many kinds of ecology, such as biological, zoological, anthropological, and sociological, the study of human ecology is urgent because technological development has rendered humanity capable of determining the fate of all existence, including plant and animal life. Humanity has the technology to extinguish and to enhance all life.

The study of ecology helps us to understand that we cannot continue to function as we have in the past. Our vast ecosystem cannot sustain indefinitely our exploitation of resources, inequitable distribution of resources, imbalances in power, control of resources, pollution of resources, and the persistence of the majority social group as the dominant force. The built-in restraints of the natural order and declining resources in the ecosystem require humanity to learn to live together as brothers and sisters on an interdependent basis. It is imperative for this to happen in spite of the cultural differences that seem to stand in our way.

The term *ecosystem* is peculiar to ecology. An ecosystem is composed of the physical or abiotic (nonliving) as well as the biological or biotic (living). The biotic and abiotic aspects of an ecosystem are inextricably intermixed. On the one hand the planet consists of one vast ecosystem. And, on the other hand, it comprises a multiplicity of sub-units also called ecosystems. Because an ecosystem is defined as a landscape, containing both biotic and abiotic components, we may refer to a particular species of plant or animal, a pond, a forest, or humanity itself as an ecosystem. Essential to any ecosystem is that the complex interaction of all of its components always functions as an organized whole.

When viewing the forest as an ecosystem, for example, we do not think of it merely as a stand of trees. We think of its related components, such as the soil, air, water, minerals, bacteria, trees, herbs, grass, birds, and insects. To investigate any aspect of the forest, therefore, certainly has great implications for the whole. And to have a specialized knowledge of any particular part of the forest requires one to have a generalized knowledge of the whole. Such an approach brings specialized and generalized areas of research into creative dialogue.

When viewed as an ecosystem, the human condition, including all majority and minority social groups, constitutes a world house. The term *ecology* is derived from the Greek word *oikos*, meaning "house" or "place to live." It also comes from the Greek word *logos*, meaning "discourse," "science," or "study."[50] All social groups are heirs of the world house. The fact that we must learn to live together as a large family on an interdependent basis is the challenge facing cultural pluralism. Martin Luther King, Jr., speaks to this when he says, "We have inherited a large house, a great 'world house' in which we have to live together — black and white, Easterner and Westerner, Gentile and Jew, Catholic and Protestant, Moslem and Hindu — a family unduly separated in ideas, culture and interest, who, because we can never again live apart, must learn somehow to live with each other in peace."[51] The road to peace requires a radical change in national and international social policies as they relate to majority-minority relations.

For example, it was predicted by the World Bank in its third annual world development statement that the number of people suffering from absolute poverty — approximately 780 million people at the time the report was written — would increase during the 1980s. The statement added that many developing countries would experience increasing instability during that decade. These predictions have become reality, and that has meant many emerging Third World countries have faced and will face massive discontent, misery, and disintegration. We realize, however, based on the principle of interdependence, that one-fifth of the human race cannot live in hunger, disease, degradation, and perpetual misery without placing in jeopardy the destinies of the other four-fifths.[52]

John Cobb in "Process Theology and Environmental Issues" attests that Latin Americans are reminding us that a fundamental obstacle to their particular liberation struggle is the economic colonialism of the United States. "There can be no speeding up the U.S. economy that does not retain and heighten its dependence on the international economic system that inhibits freedom in Latin America."[53] Continuing, Cobb makes the point that the increasing growth of technologically developed nations, especially the United States, speeds up the exhaustion of resources throughout the global village, intensifies the problem of waste and pollution, and increases our dependence on nuclear energy.

The time is now for humanity to manage the resources in the world house on an equitable basis, because for the first time in our brief history on the planet, we are "faced with ultimate, rather than merely local, limitations."[54] The resources in the world are not infinite; they are quite finite and limited. The only viable solution for *human* ecology is to close the gap between majority and minority social groups. The growing economic imbalance between social groups must be overcome.

Throughout the global village we are now feeling the rumblings of a "freedom explosion." Oppressed minority social groups everywhere are seeking liberation. The consciousness of these groups represents an idea whose time has come and makes this a special time in history. In the Greek language it is called *kairos*, "qualitative time." It differs from *chronos*, which refers to quantitative, linear, or clock time. *Kairos* is a special event within the course of historical events. In German it is referred to as the *Zeitgeist*, and in the English language it is called "the right time." The time for the complete freedom of all the oppressed is now.

The ecological perspective overcomes the anthropocentric slant of the hierarchical model. Rather than making the world human-centered, the ecological perspective attempts to clarify the role of humanity as an integral component within the larger ecosystem. Consequently, humanity is no longer perceived as detached from nature, thereby making nature the object of manipulation and exploitation. Whitehead says, "The false idea which we have to get rid of is that of nature as a mere aggregate of independent entities, each capable of isolation."[55] Humanity is a part of nature.

This perspective does not mean, however, that the human species is not unique. Whitehead accounts for this uniqueness in a manner that does not violate the ecological balance between humanity and nature. Viewing humanity and nature within the framework of evolutionary theory, Whitehead uses the category of abstraction to account for the uniqueness of humanity. He says, "Those characteristics of experience which separate the higher from the lower species of actualities all depend upon abstraction. The living germs are distinguished from lifeless physical activities by the abstractions inherent in their existence. The higher animals are distinguished from mere life by their abstractions, and by their use of them."[56]

3

Doing Theology in the Context of Cultural Pluralism

Theological Method and the Challenge
of Multicultural Patterns

Our task now is to see how Whitehead's method of empirical analysis suggests ways in which theological method can relate effectively to multicultural patterns.

As a technical discipline informed by scientific principles, the study of theology requires the formulation of a method. But whatever the method one chooses to employ in interpreting Christian faith, this method must remain open to reassessment. Theological method is an ongoing, not a once-and-for-all process. The things that keep the theological process moving are ever-changing circumstances.

Efforts to modify theological method in the face of these changes give witness to the ability of cultural factors to influence theological method. As with metaphysical presuppositions and scientific theories, theological methods do not develop in a vacuum. All theories are socially and culturally conditioned.

Today theological method cannot ignore the increasing presence of diverse social groups, each unique and different. These differences have profound implications for theological method. They must be reckoned with in a way that realizes their unique contributions to the Christian faith.

The task of the theologian is to interpret the content of the Christian faith in the clearest and most intelligible manner possible.[1] It is with this goal in mind that we draw out implications for theology of the presence of multicultural patterns.

George R. Stewart in *American Ways of Life* makes the acute observation that the process of cultural assimilation should not be described as "a melting pot"; rather, it should be viewed more as "transmuting pot," suggesting that the culture of ethnic social groups has been integrated and assimilated into "an idealized Anglo Saxon model."[2] The original presumption was that ethnic groups would maintain their distinct cultural identity. But as America developed a national consciousness, it geared the cultural assimilation process more in the direction of Anglo conformity.

Building on Stewart's position, Will Herberg in his *Protestant-Catholic-Jew* makes the point that regardless of the nature of the cultural forms that ethnic groups lost in the Americanization process, each group tended to maintain its distinct religious orientation. He concludes, "It is religion that with the third generation has become the differentiating element and the content of self-identification and social location."[3] Consequently, Herberg contends, the point of identification for cultural assimilation in American life today is to be found in the Protestant, Catholic, and Jewish religious sectors.

But we need to point out that racial discrimination and sexism have greatly interfered with the ability of women, Afro-Americans, American Indians, Orientals, and Hispanics to become fully assimilated into the mainline religious communities. Therefore, when we discuss Herberg's tripartite model of religio-cultural assimilation, we need to be aware of the variables that continue to make religio-cultural assimilation problematic for many minority social groups in America.

Now, why is this point of social delineation necessary? Because it has implications for determining how we approach theological method. If, for example, one took the position that upon assimilation into Protestantism or Catholicism each ethnic group became amalgamated into one idealized cultural expression of the Christian faith, one's approach to theological method would be geared more toward the conformity model. Here one's approach would manifest itself in the direction of a single monocultural style, because there would be little need to address cultural diversity in the true sense of the word. The attempt would be to perpetuate sameness and conformity in theological method as a means to achieving a fixed, preconceived, idealized notion of what the Christian faith should be.

On the other hand, if one approached the same situation with an awareness of the rich cultural and ethnic diversity present among social groups, one's approach to theological method would have to uphold and appreciate that diversity. One would need to show sensitivity to the unique contributions that, for example, women bring to the Christian faith. The situation of Afro-Americans would have to be dealt with from the perspective of their experiences of pain, suffering, and injustice. The way these groups tend to contextualize the Christian faith would need to be reckoned with.

Since each social group has its unique story to share in the context of the Christian faith, theological method has the challenging task of attempting to discover points of contact between all the stories while at the same time allowing each to express itself in its own situation.

The Usefulness of Whitehead's Analysis

Whitehead's method of empirical analysis[4] can relate to multicultural patterns in that it is descriptive in character. It begins with a description of the actual phenomenon. His method analyzes experience and functions in a manner similar to phenomenology.[5]

Whitehead describes his empirical method as speculative philosophy. I mentioned earlier how Whitehead sought to integrate coherence, logicality, applicability, and adequacy into his empirical method as necessary criteria for philosophical discourse. He likens the true method of discovery to the flight of an airplane. It begins from the ground of empirical observation; it flies into the area of generalization and speculation. It then returns for renewed observation.[6] The speculative process itself is not knowledge, but it is the tool, vehicle, or channel through which knowledge is acquired. The speculative process is grounded in empirical data in that all knowledge attained through it is tested against experience.[7] Such an approach is not only essential to philosophic and theological methods, but its relevance extends into psychological, historical, sociological, and anthropological studies as well. The descriptive analysis brings a challenge to each academic discipline; namely, it attempts to take organic pluralism seriously. In this regard we may ask, How do we describe cross-cultural patterns[8] without distorting their unique authenticity? In other words, How does a theoretician, whether employing methodologies from the humanistic, social, behavioral, or natural sciences, describe a cultural pattern or event that is different from his or her indigenous context without imposing his or her cultural biases on that event?

Here is another question to consider. When we seek to acquire knowledge of the religious dimensions present in different cultural patterns, do we seek the knowledge as a basis of control, manipulation, and domination? Or do we seek to enter into creative dialogue with the different cultural expression being described, to participate in its authenticity? The thing that influences both the attitude of the interpreter and the conclusions of the investigation is the type of methodology employed in the study. Whitehead's method of empirical analysis offers a constructive way to avoid the type of methodological distortions scholars have traditionally imposed on oppressed minority social groups.

Whitehead believes that the subject-object approach to reality has done much damage to metaphysical discourse in the Western cultural tradition. I believe that the subject-object approach has also damaged majority-minority intergroup relations. Consequently, as we think about theological discourse from the perspective of cultural pluralism, I see an urgent need to make a radical shift from the subject-object mode of thinking in doing theology to a subject-subject approach.

In the development of process metaphysics Whitehead was

keenly aware that no single problem in the history of Western philosophy has been more detrimental in metaphysical discourse than the subject-object approach. In fact, Whitehead wrote *Process and Reality* in an attempt to provide a corrective to the subject-object dichotomy. He believed that "all modern philosophy hinges about the difficulty of describing the world in terms of subject and object, substance and quality, particular and universal. The result always does violence to immediate experience."[9]

Since much of Whitehead's critique of the subject-object approach resides in his response to Plato and Aristotle, a brief discussion of their positions will be helpful.

The Subject-object Approach according to Plato and Aristotle

In the life and thought of Plato (428–348 B.C.), the systematic formulation of Greek philosophy reached unprecedented height. Prior to Plato, Greek philosophers were primarily cosmologists.[10] But with the emergence of Plato, and then with Aristotle, Western metaphysical discourse took upon itself sophisticated systematic structures. Whitehead himself remarked that all philosophy is a footnote to Plato. And although Plato's philosophical contributions have had positive implications throughout the history of Western thought, his development of the subject-object dichotomy has provoked many negative consequences. This is not to say that the subject-object approach is exclusively Platonic; aspects of it can be seen in a host of Western philosophical systems. We observed one phase of it earlier in the Newtonian materialist paradigm.

The key to the subject-object approach in Plato lies in the division he made between the spiritual and physical realms. We discussed an aspect of this earlier. The spiritual realm is transcendent and consists of ideas or forms. These ideas are the only true realities in the world. They are objective and serve as the basis for all scientific knowledge. These ideas are immaterial and supersensible. They are not subjective; nor are they conditioned by the physical world. These ideas are eternal, meaning that they have no beginning or end. They are removed from change and do not perish. The becoming of phenomena, as it relates to space and time in the physical realm, does not include ideas or forms. They are static and unchanging. The eternal ideas serve as norms or standards for things in the physical world. They represent perfection. Things in the physical world can only imitate or approximate the spiritual realm. Because these ideas are of a spiritual nature, things in the physical world are subordinate to them. All phenomena in the physical realm represent subjects and all phenomena in the spiritual realm are perceived as objects.[11] Plato makes a sharp distinction between subjects and objects. Since subjects are merely reflections of the objective world of ultimate reality, Plato's metaphysics creates a gulf between subjects and objects.

Aristotle (384–322 B.C.), the chief systematic metaphysician of ancient Greece, attempted one of the earliest corrections of Plato's bifurcation of subjects and objects. (Although we are focusing on the limitations present in Plato and Aristotle, it is important to note that Whitehead felt greatly indebted to both.) While Plato was not able to find an appropriate balance between the eternal ideas, which were perceived as spiritual, and the physical dimension, which he viewed as matter, the genius of Aristotle is his recognition that the forms of reality that correspond to the Platonic notion of ideas do not mutually exclude things in the physical realm.

In Aristotle's metaphysics these ideas are never separate and distinct from the physical realm; rather, each concrete thing in the physical realm represents a union of form and matter. Although we often think of form and matter as separate categories, Aristotle was able to show that neither one exists by itself. The only exception to this is in Aristotle's conception of God. As mentioned earlier, Aristotle conceives of God as an exception to all metaphysical principles. For him God represents pure substance, void of any matter.

Aristotle's metaphysics, often referred to as First Philosophy because it deals with the nature of being itself, systematically investigates that aspect of ultimate reality which is presupposed in everything that exists. Whereas scientific knowledge deals with particular aspects of being, metaphysics as used by Aristotle goes beyond an analysis of the experiential physical realm to include universal truths.[12]

The Platonic and Aristotelian traditions developed into two distinct schools of thought in regard to the subject-object approach. Both contained different aspects of the subject-object approach, and both have been quite influential throughout Western culture. The Platonic aspect of the subject-object dichotomy revolves around a dualistic world view; the Aristotelian aspect of it focuses on viewing subjects and objects as self-enduring, unchanging substances.

The Subject-object Approach according to Whitehead

One of Whitehead's critiques of the subject-object approach is that its interpretation and application to the final acts of experience have caused us to separate the way in which we interpret events from the events themselves. This means that persons generally perceive themselves as subjects and view phenomena in the actual world as objects, standing over and against themselves, to be interpreted. Whitehead says that there is a pragmatic defense for using the subject-object approach in language and logic, but when it is used in metaphysics, it is sheer error. When the subject-object approach becomes characteristic of the nature of ultimate reality, it becomes problematic for the interpretive process.

With advancements in technology, the scientific method, and the sciences in general, the subject-object approach in Western culture has become pervasive to the point of dominating part of our modern mentality. When we approach phenomena in the world, our tendency is to perceive ourselves as standing over against the thing being interpreted. Consequently, we relate to the phenomena as objects to be manipulated, controlled, and dominated. We attempt to assume mastery over objects. Since we view knowledge as power, we attempt to subordinate objects, making them mere tools of our ascendancy. When this approach is applied to our encounters with ethnic minorities, the consequences, naturally, are damaging.

For example, in our interpersonal relations sometimes we impose our biases and prejudices upon each other, blocking our ability to be genuine and authentic and another's ability to remain autonomous. We coerce and manipulate persons into conformity with our own biases. We control them by conditioning our acceptance on their conformity. This happens quite frequently in marital relationships, in relationships between parents and children, and in relationships between supervisors and subordinates.

Whenever one person imposes biases or prejudices upon another, depersonalizing of both results. Whenever one person affirms another, affirmation of both results. Whatever affects one person directly affects the other indirectly, so depersonalizing a person directly means depersonalizing oneself indirectly. We are all inextricably bound together in mutuality and interrelatedness. Such mutuality presupposes that persons have the right to define themselves, that they possess a sense of self-determination.

We also impose our human biases and prejudices upon nature. We call this anthropocentrism, the process of creating a human-centered world. When we fail to allow things within nature to represent and disclose themselves to us, we force them to become what we want them to be rather than what their inherent value suggests. Just like human beings, things within the world of nature have their own value, purpose, and self-worth. Only when we recognize this fact can we learn to respond to all phenomena — human and nonhuman — without coercing reality into conformity with our biases.

When the subject-object mode of thinking is incorporated into one's methodology, it leads to imposing one's presuppositions on the event being interpreted. These presuppositions can be both implicit and explicit. We need to be aware of both. In such instances, instead of allowing the authentic context of the event to unveil itself, the interpreter usually forces the event to conform to preconceived criteria of truth. We can see quite clearly just how the authentic cultural expressions of Afro-Americans, Mexican Americans, and American Indians, for instance, have suffered greatly as a result of the majority social group imposing on them preconceived criteria of cultural normativeness.

The alternative approach, which authenticates the interpreter while guarding against distorting the experience being interpreted, is the subject-subject mode of thinking. It grows out of Whitehead's method of empirical analysis. Whitehead defines subjects and objects in the following manner: "The word 'object' thus means an entity which is a potentiality for being a component in feeling; and the word 'subject' means the entity constituted by the process of feeling, and including this process."[13] The point Whitehead is establishing is there is no ontological distinction to be made between subjects and objects. The fact of the matter is that upon perishing, subjects become objects; and after objects undergo concrescence in an actual occasion, they become subjects.[14]

In eradicating the gulf between subjects and objects Whitehead paves the way for the present generation to rediscover a sense of intimacy with existence. The subject-subject mode of thinking suggests that all things in the world, including nature, are inextricably bound together. Whereas the subject-object approach establishes a monologue, the subject-subject approach rediscovers a creative dialogue.

The subject-object approach coerces, manipulates, dominates, and controls things in the world. The subject-subject approach seeks to enter into the authentic experiences of others. The subject-object approach is passive, meaning that there is no interchange between the interpreter and the event being interpreted. The event being interpreted is passive and remains merely the recipient. The subject-subject approach is dynamic and establishes mutuality. It is open. The subject-object approach is closed.[15]

When we discuss the sources of theology, we will see more clearly the implications of the subject-subject mode of thinking for cultural pluralism.

We must refrain, however, from making our methodologies normative. Although theological method has been described by Bernard Lonergan as "a normative pattern of recurrent and related operatives yielding cumulative and progressive results,"[16] we need to resist the tendency to become so rigid and fixed in presuppositions that they close out our capacity to affirm truths in other cultural traditions that might not conform to our own. Since a theological method is an instrument or a process by which we interpret the Christian faith, there is always room to improve upon its capacity to make truths intelligible. If we fail to maintain this kind of openness, we will increase the risk of distortion when we attempt to apply a particular theological method to social groups that have a cultural orientation to faith that is different from our own.

The Implications of Cultural Pluralism
for Interpreting the Sources of Theology

Experience

Experience is basic to interpreting the sources of theology because it is the vehicle or channel through which the sources communicate to us. It is also the medium and context through which we receive the sources.[17] Human experience, therefore, is our touchstone for understanding all knowledge. This is not to say, however, that all knowledge is exhausted in human experience; rather, it means, as Whitehead puts it, that all efforts to attain knowledge begin with an analysis of particular acts of experience. These acts of experience presuppose human experience as primary. In the quest for truth we may speculate, generalize, and form working hypotheses about unknown possibilities, but we always return to human experience to determine the reliability of the hypotheses. In a real sense, human experience is a testing ground for truth.

It is important to note that religious experience necessarily goes beyond the confines of generally accepted verification principles.[18]

At this point, I want to reflect critically upon the nature of the Christian faith in reference to the way human experience expresses itself in the context of majority-minority intergroup relations. First, I shall identify some of the sociocultural factors that have caused the traditional approaches to distort human experience. Second, I shall suggest an alternative approach that constitutes a pluralistic model for theological discourse.

Human experience is not some abstract, idealized, perfect essence removed from concrete manifestations in history.[19] The tragedy of Plato's idealistic anthropology is its creation of a dichotomy between perfect humanity, as an idea removed from the historical process, and actual humanity existing in community. Within the Platonic tradition all manifestations of human experience are perceived solely as emulations of perfect humanity, which exists in the heavens. Human experience in history can never, according to this philosophy, integrate actuality and potentiality; it can only approximate such an integration.

But we know that human experience is inclusive, not dualistic. It is socially related. It consists of a dynamic, complex organism that always integrates potentiality and actuality in history. Consequently, we abandon any notion of human experience as an abstract, idealized phenomenon objectified in a transcendent realm; rather, we say that human experience is grounded in the historical process — although, at this point, we must also add that human experience always integrates phenomena from both the vertical and horizontal dimensions of existence. Because human experience manifests itself in socio-historical activities such as language, ideas, beliefs, customs, and social organization, it acquires a cultural heritage. It is through the sociocultural context that human experience is transmitted. Also, on the basis of this transmission, as it is reflected in art, government, education, tradition, science, and the like, we abstract from historical processes specific and generalized notions of human experience.

Now, when we turn to an analysis of human experience in the context of majority-minority intergroup relations in America, we find that since the inception of Anglo conformity and the erection of the color-line barrier, Afro-Americans, one of the oldest ethnic minority social groups in America, have been trying to attain full membership into the category of human experience. Whereas Afro-Americans have always realized their true humanity, which they affirm in their experiences of God, social structures in America, including religious institutions, have never been willing to accept the Afro-American experience as an integral part of human experience. The same thing applies to American Indians and other nonwhite ethnic minority social groups. When a normative approach to human experience functions in society, it makes cultural pluralism dysfunctional.

An alternative approach that I think moves us more in the direction of cultural pluralism is the organic atomistic model.[20] I do not mean the type of atomism that exists in the old Newtonian paradigm. We have observed its problematic features in an earlier discussion. Because the Newtonian model defines experience as closed, separate, individualized, and self-contained it is not viable as a methodology for cultural pluralism. But if we view the atomistic model as an open system containing interrelated and interconnected components, as Whitehead does, it can serve as a viable model for cultural pluralism.

Within the organic atomistic model, cultural relativism becomes affirmed as a fundamental part of what it means to exist in society. And when we begin to think about this theologically, we must start explicating in more detail the diverse aspects of human experience. It is one thing to say, as Paul Tillich does, that theology begins with anthropology.[21] But more important is interpreting human experience from a pluralistic perspective. By this I mean that no perspective should become normative in defining the nature of human experience and its relation to God. We must remain open to the rich diversity that exists in each cultural tradition and within each faith community. Because human experience by its nature is pluralistic — not monolithic — we should realize that affirming its differences builds unity. Pluralism becomes a threat to unity only when any member of the community becomes closed. Closedness makes organic pluralism impossible.

The organic atomistic model recognizes that each person is interrelated with the experience of others both internally and externally. This is not to suggest that we should sacrifice our distinct individualities. But it means that as social groups maintain their distinct individualities, none can afford to assert a closed nationalism. Open nationalism affirms the experience of each particular social group while also considering the concerns of others; closed nationalism fails to embrace universalism. It adheres solely to provincialism. But open nationalism is both particular and universal.

Insights from Martin Luther King, Jr., help to illustrate the meaning of an organic atomistic approach to human experience. For centuries, he says, humankind has lived by the notion that "self-preservation is the first law of life." But this premise is built on a false assumption. King feels that the preservation of the other is the first law of life. One cannot preserve himself or herself without being concerned about the preservation of others. The structure of the universe is such that the oppression of any social group creates ecological imbalances that are harmful to all. "The self cannot be self without other selves. Self-concern without other-concern is like a tributary that has no outward flow to the ocean."[22]

When Anglo-Americans no longer put forward their experience as the norm we will be able to actualize the ideal of social interdependence between majority and minority social groups. "Whether we realize it or not each of us lives eternally in the red. We are everlasting debtors to known and unknown men and women."[23]

Revelation

In the discussion of the empirical method and its significance for interpreting multicultural patterns, I sought to set the stage for interpreting the sources of theology; toward that end I also identified some of the inadequacies present in the subject-object mode of thinking. I advocate the subject-subject approach as an alternative because it creates the occasion for the authentication of the event being interpreted. The process becomes self-authenticating for the interpreter as well as for the event being interpreted. I tried to show how the subject-subject approach can protect theological method from the danger of theological imperialism.

Although Paul Tillich rightly reminds us that theological imperialism and provincialism are as dangerous as political imperialism,[24] he concerns himself only with the intellectual aspect of the problem.

His important work *Theology of Culture*, for example, recounts his removal from his professorship at the University of Frankfurt after the victory of the Nazis in Germany. He subsequently accepted an invitation to join the faculty at Union Theological Seminary in New

York City. One of his great difficulties in leaving Germany was his doubt about being able to do his philosophical and theological work in any part of the world other than Germany. This is what Tillich means by the term *provincialism*. After working at Union and other seminaries, he became convinced that he could indeed do his work in places other than Germany. He began to feel his provincialism disappear.

Now, let me raise three questions: To what extent did theological provincialism, as it relates to the Eurocentric perspective, disappear in Tillich's lifetime? To what extent did it disappear in his own thinking? And are the presuppositions present in the Eurocentric perspective viable for cultural pluralism? I think it is important to address these questions briefly before continuing the discussion of revelation because they certainly have serious implications for how we interpret revelation.

During the span of Tillich's philosophical and theological career, both in Germany and America, modern theological discourse was dominated by the Eurocentric perspective. In fact, modern theology in large measure was shaped almost exclusively by the prevailing Eurocentric liberal perspective of the nineteenth century. Among the key figures in this period were Kant, Feuerbach, Marx, Hegel, Schleiermacher, Harnack, Kierkegaard, and Troeltsch.

The liberal Eurocentric theological perspective dominated theological discourse up until the publication of Karl Barth's epoch-making volume *Epistle to the Romans* during the early part of the twentieth century. And although Barth lifted liberal theology out of a fixation with anthropocentrism, he too wrote from the Eurocentric perspective.

So although Tillich himself may have recovered from a certain provincialism, theological discourse continues to exalt the Eurocentric perspective.

The critical issue, then, is whether the Eurocentric perspective by its nature can avoid tendencies toward provincialism, ethnocentrism, and imperialism. Can its presuppositions allow room for the wide range of experiences present among multicultural social groups? We have seen the dangers of Hegelian evolutionary theism as demonstrated by Hegel's nineteenth-century bias against Africans and Afro-Americans. How can this kind of problem, for example, be avoided in shaping world views? My point here is that it is not sufficient merely to agree with Tillich about the dangers of provincialism. We need to examine critically the presuppositions upon which the Eurocentric perspective is shaped in light of their viability for relating effectively to multicultural social groups.

As we approach the category of revelation, we need to be equally cautious about compartmentalizing God's self-manifestation into a rigid subject-object mode of thinking. Instead, because revelation by its nature has a giftlike quality, meaning that humanity cannot earn it, the appropriate posture that we should take toward revelation is one of total openness and vulnerability to God. Such a posture cannot be attained through coercive, rigid means. It cannot be attained through manipulation. It is acquired through the faith community. It involves a participatory relationship between God and humanity. It is not a monologue. Humanity is the recipient of God's gift of revelation. This makes revelation dynamic and inclusive.

I think the subject-subject approach to the experience of revelation is conducive to engaging multicultural patterns and diverse religious traditions in a common religious quest in a way that overcomes the dangers of religious imperialism. The subject-subject approach can do this because it presupposes the relativity and multidimensionality of God's revelation. We cannot assign God's self-disclosure exclusively to any particular social group; nor can we confine it to any particular religious tradition.

The subject-subject approach to the experience of revelation is based on the notion that a partnership exists between God and humanity. And an important presupposition operative here is that the principle of identity characterizes the divine-human encounter, rather than the principle of paradox.[25] This makes a fundamental difference.

The principle of paradox and the principle of identity represent two distinct traditions in the history of Christian theology. I think the principle of identity is more conducive to attaining cultural pluralism because it overcomes the type of dualistic world view that keeps Christian theologians from taking seriously the dynamic, pluralistic metaphysical categories in the world. The principle of paradox maintains the traditional Platonic split between God and the world.

The Principle of Identity

One of the early attempts to overcome the subject-object approach to God in contemporary theology, as it relates to revelation, was made by Friedrich Ernst Daniel Schleiermacher (1768–1834), often cited as the father of modern theology. Employing the principle of identity, which perceives God as the creative ground of the world, Schleiermacher attempted to overcome our tendency to think of ourselves as subjects on the one hand while projecting God as existing out there in the form of an object on the other hand. Paul Tillich describes it this way: "Here I am, the subject, and over there is God, the object. He is merely an object for me, and I am an object for him."[26]

The principle of identity, which overcomes this subject-object split for Schleiermacher, designates the presence of God within the individual. Schleiermacher defines God as the feeling of absolute dependence. This idea of feeling is not to be identified as merely subjective emotion. It is the impact of ultimate reality upon the individual to the extent that the individual becomes immediately aware of the presence of God. This immediate awareness is revelatory in character and transcends the subject-object distinction. The revelatory experience here is not supernaturalistic but experiential and empirical.

The focus of revelation in Schleiermacher's framework is a profound awareness of the presence of the ground of being, of which the self is an extension. The revelatory experience contains both a recognition of God's presence and an openness to being unconditionally dependent upon God.

Paul Tillich developed his systematic theology with an abiding appreciation of Schleiermacher's contribution. He thought that Schleiermacher's use of the phrase "God is a feeling of absolute dependence" was unfortunate in that his critics accused him of psychologism. Therefore, Tillich changed the phrase to "ultimate concern and ground of being";[27] but they mean essentially the same thing. Tillich shared much of Schleiermacher's effort to rescue theology from the subject-object approach because he believed that the revelatory character peculiar to the subject-object approach depersonalized the individual, in that it deprived the self of individuality.[28]

I think Schleiermacher's insight here is important, as is Tillich's integration of it, despite Karl Barth's criticism that the principle of identity results in anthropocentrism, which Barth characterized as the problem of liberal nineteenth-century Protestant theology. But I think the principle of identity in process thought has important implications in regard both to cultural pluralism and to revelation.

The principle of identity does not mean that theology is dissolved into anthropology. In other words, the reality of God and the nature of humanity are not amalgamated in the experience of revelation. But it means that the spiritual and the spatial are two distinguishing aspects of an integrated whole. And, although revelation transcends the immediacy of both space and time in that the past is retained in God's infinite memory and the future is imbued with inexhaustible possibilities, revelation is always available existentially in the immediate present. The goal here is that we do not disjoin God's revelation and the spatial. The principle of identity means that there is an ontological interdependence between God and humanity. The context for perceiving this sense of God's self-disclosure can be found in Whitehead's vision of novelty.

In both God's primordial and consequent natures God functions as the ground of novelty. Novelty suggests that each event is different, unique, and special. Every event represents a synthesis of many possibilities into oneness. This uniqueness makes each event a miracle and a mystery. The implication here is that when social groups are deliberately kept away from becoming fully self-actualized, we distort God's self-disclosure in history. The way to optimize God's self-disclosure in history is to embrace genuine openness and vulnerability toward all social groups. Consequently, to make any aspect of human experience the norm distorts the mystery or novelty of God's presence, which is hidden in the depths of creaturely existence.

Much of the Afro-American religious heritage, for example, represents the novelty and mystery that Whitehead describes as the creative advance of the world. But the structures in American society have yet to become genuinely open to this dimension of God's self-disclosure. The existence of cultural normativeness in America continues to prevent the type of creative integration of God's self-disclosure that is possible between the majority social group and ethnic minority social groups. The exclusion of women from full participation in social structures is another indication of how we distort God's self-disclosure. The rich expressions of spirituality in the indigenous experience of American Indians are another novelty that we have yet to appreciate. I could mention many similar examples. My point is that the issue is not whether God's self-disclosure is available to humanity but whether we are willing to recognize God's presence.

I think process thought points us in the right direction because, for example, in God's primordial nature God facilitates the self-actualization of all possibilities in the world. Without the primordial nature of God, there would be no novelty. Unless possibilities can realize themselves, novelty is both impossible and a meaningless category. We will see in the next chapter just how Whitehead intentionally avoids making God coercive in directing possibilities in the world, but for now I want to affirm the fact that novelty, mystery, difference, and diversity represent manifestations of the nature of God's self-disclosure in history. And all of this takes place in a manner that grounds it in unity rather than chaos. Because God directs these possibilities, God functions as the principle of concretion. This means that God is the principle of limitation in the world. This is the reason why there is order, not chaos, in the world.

Many think that emphasizing the multidimensional character of God's self-disclosure leads to chaos. For many people, whenever God's self-disclosure fails to manifest itself according to their understanding, the consequence is chaos. They think of God's self-disclosure singularly, while diversity or multiplicity or variety simply spells chaos. They fail to recognize that God's self-disclosure is inclusive of diversity. Multidimensionality suggests difference in degree, not in quality. For them, employing the principle of unity in diversity as a framework for God's self-disclosure makes the nature of God's revelation self-contradictory.

In other words, the manner in which God discloses Godself at a particular time in history may appear to contradict God's prior activity. But maintaining the new *gestalt*, the larger, inclusive vision of God's multidimensionality, takes one out of such narrowness and one-sidedness. That new vision is imperative to enable minority social groups to participate fully in the self-disclosure of God in history.

No particular social group or religious denomination can exhaust the magnitude of God's self-disclosure. The concept of the multidimensionality of God's self-disclosure attempts to capture such an insight. The principle of unity in conformity, on the other hand, violates the nature and character of God's self-disclosure and should be repudiated.

Hence, I think the multidimensional character of God's self-disclosure leads to order and unity. Further, it is clear that the principle of unity in conformity does not encourage novelty and mystery. It shuts them out. It does not allow multicultural diversity to unveil itself. The image of the primordial nature of God sets the stage for overcoming the problem of unity in conformity in that the very nature of God's relation to the world includes pluralism, not monocentrism. Whitehead says, "It is to be noted that every actual entity, including God, is something individual for its own sake; and thereby transcends the rest of actuality. And also it is to be noted that every actual entity, including God, is a creature transcended by the creativity which it qualifies."[29]

Because the completion of novelty takes place in the life of each creature that reaches self-actualization, and God's self-disclosure is an integral part of the total process, we can say that God is the beginning and the end of mystery and novelty. And God does this in a way that does not violate creaturely freedom. In other words, God does not superimpose novelty upon creatures. Rather, God's role is to facilitate the novelty already present in the nature of each creature. While in one sense God and all creatures are inclusive, meaning that God participates actively toward their self-actualization, in another sense, we can say that God and each creature's novel expression are mutually exclusive.[30] By this I mean that God respects the novelty inherent in each creature. God does not dominate this novelty.

When the novelty of each creature is realized, it becomes a permanent part of God's memory, which is contained in God's consequent nature. In God's consequent nature the uniqueness and value of each creature in the world are affirmed. And since God's self-disclosure takes place in events, the task of persons is to allow the novelty and mystery of God's beauty to be disclosed through these events. The variety of cultures represents the diversity of God's beauty. The task of social institutions should be to encourage such rich diversity.

While Paul Tillich's integration of Schleiermacher's principle of identity anticipated the subject-subject mode of expression found in Whitehead's process thought, Tillich's tendency to locate the nature of God outside the category of existence makes his proposal limited in regard to cultural pluralism. Although there are significant and valuable existential and phenomenological dimensions to Tillich's theological program, it fails to overcome the problem that arises when we make God an exception to all metaphysical categories.

In his effort to rescue God-talk from subject-object expression, Tillich conceived of God's beingness in a manner that makes God's nature removed from the split between subject and object distinctions. In process thought these distinctions are two aspects of one and the same process. Whitehead succeeds in integrating them. Because Tillich viewed existence as estranged and alienated, meaning that it consists of a mixture of existential and essential being, he felt that God must necessarily possess a degree of ontological significance that transcends the category of existence. The answers to the questions emerging from estrangement, he says, must come from beyond existence. These answers come from God because God transcends the category of existence while at the same time serving as the creative ground of being. Existence, therefore, participates in the creative ground of being, but God does not participate in existence alongside other subjects.[31]

Reason, for instance, constitutes the question of estrangement for us because reason is grounded in the limitations of creaturely existence. Because reason is grounded in that way, revelation, the answer to this question, must come from beyond existence. Tillich uses such categories as ecstasy, mystery of being, and miracle to convey his understanding of revelation. In fact, he feels that revelation means the self-disclosure of the mystery of that which concerns us ultimately. It comes to us through a miracle, and when we experience it, the process can be described as an ecstasy of the mind.

By mystery Tillich is pointing to that dimension which is hidden in reality. It refers to the unique quality of a thing, which is often obscured. The mysterious character of ultimate concern is its power to conquer nonbeing, as well as its capacity to add meaning to existence in spite of its ambiguities. While the question, What does it mean to be? on the negative side contains the shock or threat that nonbeing is a real possibility; on the positive side the mystery of ultimate concern suggests that all anxiety and questions related to finite limitations are overcome by the power of ultimate concern.

Ecstasy means that the mind transcends itself and stands outside itself. This is the point at which, while including an emotional experience, reason through the intellect transcends the subject-object distinction without rejecting itself. Miracle does not suggest, for Tillich, an extraordinary event that defies the laws of nature; rather, it represents the manner in which the mystery of being is revealed to us, which takes place in ordinary events in history.[32]

An important element in process theism, which goes beyond the limitations of Tillich, is the fact that God is made of the same stuff as all other phenomena in the world. All phenomena consist of actual entities, including God. According to Whitehead, the description of the generic character of actual entity should include God as well as the lowliest actual occasion, though there is a specific difference between the nature of God and that of any occasion. The point here is that in all metaphysical categories, God is the chief exemplification. There are no exceptions, says Whitehead. Now, why is this important for cultural pluralism?

What God's Self-disclosure Means for Pluralism

The central problem in the way cultural pluralism manifests itself in America today is the fact that Afro-Americans, women, American Indians, and many other minority social groups are not fully integrated into social institutions. They remain marginalized. A social conception of God, as developed in process theism, opens the door for oppressed social groups to develop strategies of social change geared toward eradicating the causes of exclusion. In the process system of thought, God meets oppressed persons in their particular context, identifies with them, and provides for them the kind of existential caring, nurture, and affirmation needed to motivate them toward the transformation of social ills. The transformation process itself contains elements of God's self-disclosure. God's role is not to transform society for us. Rather, God participates with us in the transformation process. More will be said about this later.

The Afro-American religious experience is one that recognizes the multidimensionality of God's revelation in history. Earlier in this book we saw the way in which W. E. B. Du Bois spoke to this matter. In dealing with the problem of cultural normativeness, on the one hand, and realizing the cultural distinctiveness of Afro-Americans, on the other hand, Du Bois reminds us that the larger religious experience of America also has important contributions to make to the development of culture.

Predominantly white mainline religious denominations have either neglected or belittled the authentic revelatory experiences of ethnic minority members because they do not fit the accepted pattern. But these revelatory experiences represent gifts from God to the human condition. My hope is that mainline churches will rise to the challenge of integrating these gifts into the core of their denominational philosophies in an effort to overcome the problem of marginality. No one ethnic group and no particular denomination can have a monopoly on God's revelation in history. It is much too vast for such confinement.

Scripture

The Bible is an important source of Christian theology because it is the original document that records the revelatory experiences upon which the Christian faith was founded. The Bible itself is not revelation. God's revelation always takes place in historical events, and actual experiences. The Bible consists of the record of revelatory experiences in the context of the faith community.[33] However, we must bear in mind that God's revelation did not terminate in the events experienced by the founders of the faith community. While the revelatory experiences of the founders of the faith should always remain the primary basis upon which the contemporary faith community lives out its commitment, we must remain open to God's self-disclosure in present situations.

When multicultural social groups use the Bible as a historical reference point for anchoring their respective faith communities, several issues related to exegesis and hermeneutics arise. One way or another these issues tend to focus on interpreting the historic context of the faith community and showing its relevance to the contemporary situation.

For women, for example, these issues are related to the problem of sexism, an issue that men need to be concerned about as well. How does one relate contemporary concerns about sexism, language, racism, and the status and role of women in relation to men to the ancient texts of the Bible?

The historical-critical method is important and should be employed in our examination of the ancient biblical texts because it makes us aware and appreciative of the Bible's original socio-historical context. Efforts to get behind the texts in quest of historical facts are to be affirmed. It is difficult to try to obtain objective facts about ancient texts that were not written according to the canons of modern historiography. Rudolf Bultmann's demythologizing methods represent a major achievement in dealing with this problem.

Although many disagree with Bultmann's conclusions, and for valid reasons, the dilemma he posed to us in regard to relating the biblical cultural context to the modern cultural context remains of pressing concern as we begin to take cultural pluralism seriously. The difference is that for Bultmann the modern cultural context was perceived solely from the Eurocentric perspective.

Today we realize that the modern culture is far more diverse, consisting of a conglomeration of multicultural perspectives. The Eurocentric perspective represents one approach alongside a growing host of others, including those coming from the Third World.

Bultmann begins his demythologizing with the assertion that the whole world view upon which the New Testament is structured contains mythological imagery rather than objective facts. Examples of this mythological imagery are: (1) the three-story structure of the world — earth, heaven, and hell; (2) the intervention of supernatural powers in the course of historical events; (3) the conception of miracles; (4) demon possession; and (5) the idea that the world although created by God is ruled by Satan or the devil.[34]

Because the mythological imagery of the New Testament is incompatible with the modern scientific world view, Bultmann proposed the process of demythologizing as a way of getting to the deeper meaning behind the mythological conception. The purpose of demythologizing, he says, "is not to eliminate the mythological statements but to interpret them. It is a method of hermeneutics."[35]

There is obviously a great danger involved in imposing presuppositions from our modern scientific culture on the world view of the founders of the faith. But the ancient biblical texts must maintain relevance for the ever-changing circumstances of modern humanity. As we attempt to make the connection between the Bible and our situation, we must try to avoid distorting the Bible's authentic context.

Retrieving the Bible's Relevance

Regardless of the problems involved with unanswered questions about the authentic and inauthentic sayings of Jesus, with the quest for the historical Jesus, and with other aspects of New Testament research, we need to find creative ways of allowing the context of the Bible to speak to our present situation. We must establish a creative dialogue with the ancient texts. In this way the truths contained in the revelatory events recorded in the Bible can interface with God's continued self-disclosure in our particular situation. In this way the ancient texts communicate to us, and our particular situation communicates with them.

Although it is not possible to interpret events without presuppositions, since interpreters always bring along their biases, it is possible through the subject-subject approach, as I have attempted to point out, to bracket our presuppositions to the extent that the authentic ethos of each cultural context will re-present itself to the interpreter.

While in one sense I want to affirm Bultmann's emphasis on human existence as primary in his hermeneutical approach, in another sense I want to view it critically. His Eurocentric approach to human existence is much too narrow to be applicable to multicultural social groups that do not necessarily share the presuppositions undergirding his understanding of human existence. While I realize that each person has to speak from his or her particular perspective, and the Eurocentric perspective happens to be Bultmann's, I am suggesting that when we speak about human existence today we should recognize its pluralistic dimensions. Human existence today manifests itself in diverse cultural forms, which require different approaches to both hermeneutics and exegesis.

Otherwise we will overlook the novelty and mystery present in each social group, and our methodological categories will still not be based on the unique features of each group. Bultmann's approach to human existence tends to be monocentric; it is not pluralistic.

As we think about human existence today we realize that one form of it consists of the lives of a relatively small number of persons who live within a few powerful nations and who possess a capitalist, corporate, entrepreneurial mentality that is committed to status, power, and the control of existing natural and human resources. And, on the other hand, we have oppressed victims of power and control, such as black South Africans, women, Afro-Americans, Latin Americans, and American Indians. Biblical exegesis from the perspective of cultural pluralism will enable us to show sensitivity to the diverse social groups. It will also allow each social group to form its unique interpretation of the biblical categories in light of its situation. Although each social group will be concerned with such basic issues as social justice, spirituality, liberation, salvation, and social transformation, being more inclusive will enable us to meet people where they are; and the only way we can do this is to become more open to their particular situations as we engage in exegetical and hermeneutical analysis.

This means further that each social group comes to the biblical text with its unique set of questions; these questions might vary from the original intent of the text. This challenges Bultmann's understanding of the criteria and validation of the method of interpreting the text. He thinks that the questions we bring to the text should coincide with the questions the text itself seeks to answer. But the complexity of the plight of the oppressed today is such that their questions cannot be forced to coincide with the questions the text is seeking to answer.

My critique of Bultmann's approach to Scripture and hermeneutics has similarities to the concerns I raised about Paul Tillich and the Eurocentric world view. I reintroduce these concerns here to remind us that the cultural ethos of the Eurocentric perspective needs to be re-examined in light of challenges from Afro-Americans and other minority social groups; one of those challenges is that Scripture interpretation relate effectively to the requirements of cultural pluralism.

We must also recognize that the ancient texts themselves represent diversity and pluralism. They integrate various cultural traditions. This implies the principle of unity in diversity in the Bible rather than a monocentric type of conformity.

My point here is that when questions of exegesis and hermeneutics are raised from the perspective of oppressed minority social groups, their viability cannot be affirmed if we insist that the narrow Eurocentric perspective is the only legitimate one for interpreting

Scripture. An integration of insights from various cultural traditions and world views will foster a larger range of options in approaching Scripture. The way to make this happen is to discover the historical roots of each ethnic cultural tradition and to take each culture seriously.

Tradition

Tradition is very much related to Scripture. After a certain methodological approach has persisted for a long time in a particular faith community, it usually becomes an integral part of tradition. Tradition serves a vital function in the life of each faith community. But later I will also point out an aspect of tradition that needs to be avoided.

Tradition protects the community of faith against thoroughgoing individualism. This is not to say, however, that we do not take the value of each individual seriously. It means that tradition sustains the corporate life force of the community. The real challenge is to find an appropriate balance between the individual and the corporate life of the faith community. Tradition holds members of the faith community accountable to its teachings, beliefs, and presuppositions. In other words, no member of the faith community has the right to pursue a particular doctrine that would bring anarchy or chaos to the faith community. Tradition holds the faith community in a type of check-and-balance system. For instance, if a member of the faith community develops a particular approach to Scripture that is contrary to the tradition established by the community, it is the task of the community itself to raise serious objections to such interpretation. This is the type of safeguard the faith community has created within its own corporate life to protect the community against potentially disintegrating influences.

Tradition gives to each faith community a sense of identity. It gives definition, purpose, reason for being, and a solid foundation. Tradition helps the community to understand and appreciate its past and present. Only on the basis of such an appreciation can the faith community move together to face the uncertainties of the future. Often both the present and future directions of the faith community stem from a growing awareness of its tradition. Based on an identification of those elements of the tradition that have sustained the life and vitality of the faith community, it can redefine itself when necessary and set forth new directions. Usually these sustaining elements are rehearsed or recited over and over again before the faith community makes any major decision about redefining itself.

This is why it is so necessary for each faith community to share its rich tradition constantly through storytelling. Storytelling reminds the members of their identity and purpose. It also serves as an excellent way to assimilate and acculturate new members. Storytelling is at its best in small group settings, where mutual sharing is encouraged.

Tradition also serves as a reservoir for cultural forms peculiar to a particular faith community. Each social group perpetuates its own indigenous cultural expressions through its religious traditions. The black church in America is a prime example of this. Despite efforts to force Afro-Americans to abandon their unique cultural heritage, the black religious experience, disseminated through what the noted sociologist E. Franklin Frazier called the invisible and institutional black church, preserves their cultural heritage. For example, our memory is sustained through storytelling. During years of slavery, when white oppressors sought systematically to erase all authentic African cultural expressions from the lives of Afro-Americans, storytelling and oral tradition preserved these Africanisms. The entire body of literature characterizing the Afro-American tradition affirms this truth, and the Afro-American community continues to manifest this insight.

Sermons within the Afro-American religious tradition have also always adhered to storytelling. Not only do they speak of moral values, dignity, self-worth, and self-esteem, but they also constantly remind the community of its historical roots, including the experience of Africa, slavery, and the quest for freedom. The spirituals as well as secular music continue to serve such a function. Through storytelling and oral tradition the vitality of faith and religious commitment has been sustained through the history of Afro-Americans.

A similar pattern can be found among American Indians and other oppressed minority social groups.

In one sense the Christian faith consists of one big tradition. But in another sense it consists of a plurality of traditions and indeed many different social groups. Although there needs to be some form of unity in doctrine and teachings, there also needs to be an openness to the particular needs, values, and concerns of each social group.

One aspect of tradition, however, poses a danger. This is its tendency to become closed to new possibilities. Tradition can stagnate a faith community. And when stagnation sets in, change is resisted. Each faith community inevitably encounters weaknesses and inherent inadequacies. Consequently, each member should never cease to challenge the community to rethink its belief systems. Such is the prophetic task, which should characterize the life-style of each member of the faith community, not just the clergy and theologians.

To counteract this potential danger, the people of God should continually scrutinize tradition, assessing its strengths and weaknesses. Otherwise the faith community runs the risk of acting irresponsibly before the demands of the Gospel of Jesus Christ. When it appears that the faith community is not consistent with the requirements of the Gospel, it should be challenged from within to reaffirm its strengths on the one hand and to move beyond its weaknesses on the other hand. Dietrich Bonhoeffer, Martin Luther, the prophet Amos, and most recently Martin Luther King, Jr., took this kind of action.

King, for example, successfully challenged American tradition. Even though segregation was accepted by both secular and religious institutions, King heeded dictates of his conscience and building upon America's creed of freedom, Gandhi's philosophy of nonviolence, the Christian faith, and the tradition of protest movements of the black church,[36] he brought about the repudiation of the era of segregation and ushered in the era of integration. If King had been too tradition-bound, he would not have voiced the prophetic message that God had for this generation.

Sexism, racism, imperialism, classism, and cultural normativeness have become, in many ways, institutionalized in our life-style.

They have become a part of American tradition. For many they are accepted truths of God. Only by the faith community's commitment to social justice, a commitment rooted in the principle of unity in diversity, will these traditions be challenged, thus making genuine cultural pluralism a reality in America.

The Afro-American religious experience generally and the theology of Martin Luther King, Jr., in particular illustrate how tradition can be used creatively and redemptively. King, for example, recognized that the basic truths inherent in the Christian faith affirm pluralism and oppose segregation defined on the basis of racial superiority. King used the prophetic element of protest peculiar to the Afro-American experience to challenge this unsound tradition of segregation. Becoming bound to tradition denies the transforming power that is so basic to the Christian faith.

Within the context of the Whiteheadian model, the type of challenge that King brought to tradition represents the expression of emerging novelty in the human condition, which creates necessary tension between the present and the not-yet. This eschatological tension has always characterized the Christian faith.

In the past advocates of Christian pluralism have suggested that the churches of Afro-Americans, American Indians, Hispanics, and other minority social groups have needed the contributions of the white church; those advocates have not been willing to affirm the white church's need of contributions from the traditions of minority churches.

Cultural pluralism calls for a reconstruction not only of religion in America but of the nature of church history.

Church History and Culture

American church historians (to say nothing of those who work in other academic disciplines) are faced with the urgent task of taking account of all social groups when they interpret the development of religion in this country. The typical approach has been to allow the majority social group to predominate in determining the interpretation of the data. Historians have concentrated on and celebrated the many contributions that members of the majority social group have made in shaping religion in America. But they have treated the contributions of Afro-Americans and other minority social groups as isolated incidents. They have failed to integrate them fully into the study of church history in America.[37]

There is, obviously, an important place for the specialized study of the contributions made by distinct ethnic groups in shaping religion in America. This helps each social group to understand its own role in making America what it is today and gives it a feeling of worth, pride, and identity. Therefore, academic courses exploring these distinct contributions should be encouraged. But this alone is insufficient. We need also to find creative ways of integrating these diverse contributions into the basic methodologies that inform our approach to the study of church history in America, and church history in general. For example, in religious education, regardless of the ethnic composition of the particular church, every effort should be made to assist people in understanding the many contributions that minority social groups have made in shaping religion in America and throughout the global village. The literature which we use in religious education should be exemplary of cultural and ethnic diversity and should model the kind of new ethnic consciousness which it is going to take to make theological, social, and cultural pluralism a genuine reality in America.

Inclusiveness in religious education will change racial attitudes, stereotypes, biases, and prejudices. It will help people at least to understand that majority social groups stand alongside a host of minority social groups in shaping religion in America and the world. Majority groups do not stand as normative. Such an orientation would help people to reconceive their relation to others. Perceiving oneself as existing alongside another is fundamentally different from perceiving oneself at the head or at the top. And since religious value formation is determinative in cultural conditioning, it provides an essential point of departure for fostering social pluralism.

If we embraced the principle of unity in diversity rather than unity in conformity in the study of church history, we would realize the inherent danger involved in taking a normative cultural

approach. Cultural pluralism requires the consideration of all social groups. This entails allowing their authentic perspectives to be
voiced. We tend to make them subordinate to the prevailing interpretive scheme of the majority social group.

If the integrative approach is developed with sincerity and commitment, and if we learn a common history that has been shaped
by diverse ethnic groups, we will be able to overcome racial stereotypes and prejudice, fears, myths, and ignorance about the creative
diversity that has shaped religion in America. This would help us to
overcome the cultural isolationism that exists in America today.

The multicultural study of church history is not intended just
for minority ethnic groups. Members of the majority social group
should be as informed about the history of the black church, for
instance, as they are about the history of their own church. While
Afro-Americans and other minorities have always had to learn about
the contributions of the white church, whites have never felt the
need to be as informed about the contributions of the churches of
the ethnic minorities. Such an approach perpetuates cultural isolationism and ignores the requirements of cultural pluralism.

This integration of diversity does not amalgamate our respective ethnic differences. Indeed, it accentuates differences, for unity
heightens differentiation; it does not dissolve it.[38] This is the type
of cultural pluralism the Afro-American community envisions for
America. It comes out vividly in the words of Langston Hughes:

> O Yes,
> I say it plain,
> America never was America to me,
> And yet I swear this oath —
> America will be![39]

And in the words of Margaret Walker:

> And in the white gods of a new land we have been believers in the
> mercy of our masters and the beauty of our brothers, believing in
> the conjure of the humble and the faithful and the pure. Neither the
> slavers' whip nor the lynchers' rope nor the bayonet could kill our

Black belief. In our hunger we beheld the welcome table and in our nakedness the glory of a long white robe. We have been believers in the New Jerusalem.[40]

In its quest for cultural pluralism in America, the black church has always resisted defining such pluralism in a way that would cause Afro-Americans to lose their unique cultural heritage. In fact, we can say that the black church was born in protest to segregation and discrimination, which, being imposed upon the Afro-American community, gave rise to the formation of the institutional black church. Originally Afro-Americans attempted to worship with whites. But when they came to worship in large numbers they were banned from the services, and they started their own independent congregations. Those who were not expelled from the services were consigned to segregated sections of the church.[41]

With the exception of a few separatist movements that Afro-Americans were forced to consider,[42] the black church has pioneered in the realization of cultural pluralism in America. Despite occasions of disillusionment and despair, Afro-Americans have developed "an implicit hope in the Declaration of Independence and in the Constitution, that one day the ideas enshrined in these historic documents would be actualized and that there would arise an earthly city, a beloved community, in which they would be citizens with all the rights, prerogatives, and responsibilities with which white men were invested."[43] The quest for the beloved community is epitomized in the social philosophy of Martin Luther King, Jr.[44]

Reason

The first function that reason serves for theological discourse is to establish the uniqueness of humanity within the evolutionary process. Humanity's highly configurated consciousness gives it a special place. This is not to say, however, that humanity is set apart from the creative process. I have tried to point out earlier the detrimental effects on nature and human relations of an anthropocentric approach to the world. Rather, this special consciousness firmly links humanity to the totality of interconnected resources. Reason has both general and specific dimensions. In its general meaning, this highly developed consciousness makes humanity responsible for enhancing the life of all beings, including lower animals and nature. In referring to this, Whitehead categorizes the function of reason in a threefold manner. He says reason should help us (1) to live, (2) to live well, (3) to live better. His point is that reason enables us first to be alive; second to live in a satisfactory way; and third, to increase satisfaction or fulfillment.[45]

A pluralistic model requires us to be concerned with the quality of life of all social groups. For example, members of the majority social group should be as concerned about the social ills that perpetuate marginal existence as its victims are. Likewise, we must find an ecological balance that will enable all to maximize the quality of life, striving for an equitable distribution of resources in the world.

The particular or specific dimension of reason has to do with coherence. As mentioned earlier, one of Whitehead's major concerns in metaphysical construction is the quest for coherence, logicality, applicability, and adequacy. It is the function of reason to raise essential questions related to those doctrines, beliefs, assumptions, accepted truths, and presuppositions that are present in philosophical and theological discourse. The purpose of this is to challenge philosophical and theological systems of thought to attaining more coherence in interpreting human experience. "What persists through every doctrine about the nature of the world or God is the demand that it hold together in the light of all we know. It is the demand for an organically unifying interpretation of experience."[46]

Just as we seek coherence in metaphysical formulation, we must also seek it in practice. In other words, Whitehead gives coherence through metaphysical reason to the one and the many. Philosophical and theological discourse should preserve the one and the many. Consequently, all metaphysical systems should accept the principle of unity in diversity as fundamental to existence itself. We must also seek to realize the one and the many in social systems.

When it comes to interpreting reason from the perspective of pluralism we have to be careful about how we understand the nature and function of reason. For example, based on the traditional Eurocentric approach, our analysis of reason fails to take into account diverse cultural situations. Discussions of particularity usually presuppose the cultural normativeness of the Eurocentric perspective. And discussions of universalization based on reason usually confine the quest for conformity to the narrow presuppositions of the Eurocentric perspective. This approach manifests itself in the form of intellectual provincialism.

Different cultures have different learning styles, different idioms, and different understandings of reason. The different methodological approaches we bring to rationalism, epistemology, and the cognitive process must be sensitive to these diverse cultural perspectives. Otherwise we run the risk of perpetuating intellectual provincialism.

Considering the particularities of each culture's approach to reason will help us make our own methods more effective. As Whitehead points out, if our methods are incompatible with experience, we should modify our methods rather than modifying experience to fit our methods.

Modifying our methods includes becoming more sensitive to the various ways in which reason functions and manifests itself among minority social groups. Different styles of learning, for example, call for different methods of teaching. Women have different learning styles than men. Many Afro-Americans, Mexican Americans, and others reared in urban areas develop nontraditional learning styles. These diverse learning styles suggest the need to develop different methods in both secular and religious education.

The Importance of Redesigning Theological Language

Theological language is culturally conditioned. It always reflects the prevailing cultural ethos. Whitehead insists upon redesigning language in an effort to make metaphysical descriptions of reality more accurate. The old Newtonian paradigm of scientific materialism, for example, distorted experience by treating the abstract as though it were concrete. Shifting from the old Newtonian world view to that of neoclassical metaphysics required a revolution in metaphysical language. It necessitated a reconceptualization and a reorientation of language usage. Such paradigmatic changes call for the dismantling of traditional ways of describing things.

For example, churches should constantly review and re-examine liturgy and all published literature to eliminate sexist or racist language. This also applies to language that focuses on the disabled, on classes and races, and on hegemony. Such forms of language perpetuate dehumanization and oppression. The church should lead all social institutions in overcoming this problem. At the local, national, and international levels, all religious and social institutions could benefit from a constant reassessment of language and its usage.

As we now experience a new birth in ethnic consciousness requiring us to integrate social justice issues with cultural pluralism, we are obligated to transform traditional theological language. Sexism and racism, for example, were born and sustained under the old materialist paradigm, whose substantial, self-contained, compartmentalized, and closed categories yielded exclusionary principles that prevented minority groups from entering fully into the mainstream of all social institutions, including the Christian church.

A basic assumption underlying Whitehead's effort to redesign language in metaphysics is the recognition that all language usage inevitably does violence to immediate experience. In other words, there is always a duality between experience and interpretation or expression. We first have knowledge through acquaintance; we then seek to articulate it through description or expression.[47] Because we are limited by language itself, meaning that some degree of distortion is always inevitable, theological discourse should always include a critique of language usage.

The goal of language systems should be to describe human experience and other forms of existence as accurately as possible. Words are abstractions from the concrete. They are not the concrete. When we discover particular types of harmful words or phrases — such as those depicting Afro-Americans as inferior and others depicting women as subordinate — we must realize that they are distortions of the real and should be redesigned. Our language should enhance liberation and humanization, not perpetuate racism and sexism. This discrimination has become so ingrained in our experience that any effort to develop a more humane mode of describing experience meets resistance. There are those who would like to see the old social paradigm continued. But people of goodwill are taking seriously the task of identifying new ways of describing human experience. This shift involves, as I have said earlier, a transition from the subject-object approach to the subject-subject approach.

It is particularly important in theological discourse to avoid distorting the experiences of different social groups. Referring to God exclusively in masculine terms, for instance, creates a distortion for many women. Using both masculine and feminine language is the way to include women when speaking of God. When we describe human experience, we cannot afford to employ a mono-centric perspective, because this automatically excludes emerging Third World social groups. We must approach human experience from a pluralistic point of reference, meaning that we must abandon all inferiority-superiority designations when describing cultural patterns. Cultural pluralism requires cultural equality. Our theological language systems have to accommodate such requirements.

The need to redesign theological language is ongoing. Because theological systems are not infinite in their capacity to maintain relevance for any given era, they must be revised constantly. A failure to revise them creates a cultural lag. We cannot revise a theological system without modifying its language. And if we accept the premise that change is fundamental to what it means to be alive, we will recognize more fully that revising theological language is an essential part of doing theology.

It is important also to note that the reality of God is not removed from this process. When we seek to revise language systems to make them more accurate in describing experience, we affect the reality of God. God is not unaffected by the human condition. God's relation with the world penetrates every aspect of creaturely existence, from the most infinitesimal to the most highly configurated. Our actions in history affect God both positively and negatively.

4

The Reality of God and the Liberation of the Oppressed

God and Inclusiveness

A radical shift in paradigmatic world views requires a doctrine of God that is consistent with the basic presuppositions of that shift. The idea of God in process metaphysics is consistent with the radical shift from the closed materialist framework to an open, organic perspective. I wish to show how this view of God has implications for the liberation of oppressed social groups. Liberation from systemic forms of oppression is necessary for cultural pluralism to be realized in a way that has importance for all social groups.

In order for the idea of God to have liberating possibilities for victims of systemic oppression, God's nature must contain inclusiveness. Here I am suggesting that God's nature must include the dynamic pluralistic dimensions of finite existence. We must forsake the theistic and supernaturalistic notions about God's detachment from the changing circumstances of finite existence. We must eradicate the bias that says there is something intrinsically inferior about the dynamic and pluralistic.[1]

Consequently, such categories as change, becoming, potentiality, imperfection, temporality, relativity, and finitude must cease to
be considered secondary. In order for God to possess inclusiveness,
these categories must be a part of God. Whitehead satisfies this requirement by insisting that God is the chief exemplification of all
metaphysical categories.[2]

Because Whitehead avoids making a generic distinction between
God and other events in the world, he is able to overcome the
disjunction of God and temporal existence that was made by the
supernaturalists. In process thought God is conceived as a non-
temporal actual entity forever participating in the constant flux of
temporality. God is not an exception to all metaphysical principles.
This does not mean, however, that God does not maintain uniqueness and holiness. Rather, it means that finite realities in the world
are real and they are taken seriously by God.

A basic concern of oppressed social groups is to affirm God's
participation in their situation. Because the majority social group has
often decided what constitutes legitimate God-talk, the theological
concerns of the oppressed have often gone unheeded.

The proliferation of liberation theologies, for example, is related
to the exclusion of minority social groups from mainstream theological discourse. It is also related to a unifying principle — namely, all
oppressed social groups share the need to contextualize theological
discourse according to their unique circumstances.

The being of God includes contextualization in the sense that
God is an integral part of both the becoming and perishing of each
experience in the world. God participates in the experience of each
creature as he or she makes transitions in life from potentiality to
actuality and finally into death. God's consequent nature includes
all experiences objectively. Whitehead says, "Forms suffer changing relations; actual entities 'perpetually perish' subjectively, but
are immortal objectively. Actuality in perishing acquires objectiv-
ity, while it loses subjective immediacy. It loses the final causation
which is its internal principle of unrest, and it acquires efficient
causation whereby it is a ground of obligation characterizing the
creativity."[3] This is not to suggest, however, that God's being is lim-

ited to the totality of experiences in the world, as in pantheism. Rather, in God's primordial nature God exists apart from all experiences in the world. And in God's consequent nature God includes all experiences.

Before explaining the difference between God's primordial and consequent natures, it will be helpful to see how process theism avoids the problem of cultural normativeness. It is avoided in the sense that Whitehead denies that any experience, including God, can assume the role of absolute transcendence and absolute immanence.[4] In other words, no experience, including God, is separate, self-contained, and detached from constant influence from other experiences. The fact that God is related organically to all experiences in the world guards against any experience abstracting itself beyond ordinary experience as normative.

All notions of "manifest destiny" and "messianic nationalism" are manifestations of belief in absolute immanence and absolute transcendence. Process theism avoids both. Not only is God a "potential" for every becoming, but every experience in the world is a "potential" for God's becoming. God is affected ontologically by all events in the world and God's being effects all events. Process theism rejects all notions of abstracting the idea of absoluteness from cultural expressions. Those notions are replaced by the principles of relativity and relationality. There is no room in process theism for provincialism and ethnocentrism. The abstraction of each experience in culture at best represents the coming together of many possibilities alongside other emerging possibilities. This is found in the principle of relativity.

Because the principle of relativity asserts that God is a potential for the becoming of every finite experience in the world, God's presence cannot be compartmentalized and relegated to certain events in history at the exclusion of others. To say that God participates in certain events in history does not preclude God's involvement in others. Obviously, this brings up the need for us to deal with the problem of suffering and systemic malfunctions in the world in relation to God's participation in history. This problem will be addressed later in this chapter.

God's Primordial and Consequent Natures

Process metaphysics says that God has a primordial nature and a consequent nature, and thus it says that God is dipolar. The primordial nature refers to the transcendent pole and the consequent nature refers to God's immanence. These natures are not mutually exclusive. And they do not function in a dualistic manner. They are interdependent and complementary dimensions of God's being. In God's dipolarity God possesses both permanence and change, temporality and everlastingness, potentiality and actuality, being and becoming, self-sufficiency and dependency, perfection and imperfection, cause and effect, and so forth. Whitehead helps to clarify this in the following statements:

> It is as true to say that God is permanent and the World fluent, as that the World is permanent and God is fluent.
> It is as true to say that God is one and the World many, as that the World is one and God many.
> It is as true to say that, in comparison with the World, God is actual eminently, as that, in comparison with God, the World is actual eminently.
> It is as true to say that the World is immanent in God, as that God is immanent in the World.
> It is as true to say that God transcends the World, as that the World transcends God.
> It is as true to say that God creates the World, as that the World creates God.[5]

To say that God is dipolar means that God has a mental pole and a physical pole. And God is not alone in this. All actual entities in the world contain a mental and physical pole. The mental pole refers to the internal, and the physical pole refers to the external. Although no actual entity is devoid of either pole, there is a difference in the relative degree of importance.[6] A point of difference between God and other actual entities is that in God the mental pole is prior to the physical pole.

Whitehead makes God and the world contrasted opposites in which the ultimate principle creatively accomplishes the task of transforming the many disjointed, diverse aspects of finite existence into a sense of converging unity. Whereas traditional theists and supernaturalists created a gulf between God and the world, thereby making for a totally static God and a fluent world, Whitehead succeeds in integrating the two. God is the unity of conceptual vision always integrating itself into the world of multiplicity. And the world is the multiplicity of finite creatures always seeking a perfected unity in God. "Neither God, nor the World, reaches static completion. Both are in the grip of the ultimate metaphysical ground, the creative advance into novelty."[7]

Whitehead's integration of the primordial and consequent natures of God has profound implications for liberation. The following factors are basic to the liberationist quest: wholeness, inclusiveness, and self-identity manifested in a context that seeks to overcome sexism, racism, colonialism, and other social ills; hence, it is essential that each liberation effort considers all aspects of the human condition. By this I mean in order to take seriously the political, socioeconomic, spiritual, and psychological dimensions of existence, we must always seek to integrate the spiritual and spatial within existential history. The primordial nature of God, as free, complete, unlimited, and infinite in the resources it provides constantly to the world, functions as a safeguard against dissolving theology into anthropology, for there is always an aspect of God's spiritual presence that can never be exhausted in any event in history.

Liberation and the Integration of the Spiritual and the Spatial

What I am suggesting here is that efforts geared toward integrating all dimensions of existence, including the spiritual and spatial, into an interlocking network of mutuality and interdependence serve to point the liberation struggle in the proper direction. We cannot afford to spiritualize oppression and relegate liberation to a compensatory orientation. Oppressed persons must be challenged to find fulfillment of their physical, emotional, and spiritual needs within history. The liberation of the body and the soul are equally impor-

tant, for the spiritual and the spatial are two fundamental aspects
of a single process.

I believe that the authentic roots of the Judeo-Christian heritage,
as well as those of the African world view, are more inclined toward
an integration rather than a separation of the spiritual and spatial.[8]
Much of the division between the spiritual and spatial found in the
Judeo-Christian heritage is the result of an engrafting of Platon-
ism and Cartesianism onto Christian theology. And elements of this
separation found in the Afro-American tradition are results of the
assimilation of traditional African religious customs into Christian
forms. This took place during the evangelization of Africa by Christian missionaries in the nineteenth and early twentieth centuries.
It also resulted from the Christianization of Afro-Americans during
the modern institution of slavery.

It is important to note, however, that an orientation toward an
integration of the spiritual and spatial remained present throughout
the history of the Judeo-Christian tradition and the Afro-American
tradition in spite of the assimilation process. Consequently, we can
say that in a real sense the quest for inclusiveness, which begins with
an integration of the spiritual and spatial, on the one hand represents
a rediscovery of the authentic roots of the Judeo-Christian heritage.
And, on the other hand, it means a return to the authentic roots of
Afro-Americans.

Joseph Klausner in *The Messianic Idea in Israel* points out that
the kingdom of the Jewish Messiah contained an integration of the
political, social, and ethical. "Hence the Jewish people did not separate faith, which is spiritual, from social life, which is practical and
political."[9] The ancient Hebrew viewed the self as consisting of a
psycho-physical unity. The body, therefore, was not thought to be
a prison or tomb for the soul. The closest term for soul that was
used by the Hebrews is *nephesh*, which refers to wind or spirit. The
Hebraic use of the term is in the direction of describing the self as a
unified personality, as opposed to creating a dualism between soul
and body. The body was not considered evil. Rather, Hebraic anthropology is holistic and inclusive, thereby integrating the spiritual
and spatial.

An integration of spirit and body is also found in the New Testament. J. A. T. Robinson points out that the tension between spirit and body found in Pauline anthropology is not consistent with the type of acute dualism present in Greek thought in which evil matter is in opposition to spirit or mind. Robinson argues that the word *fleshly* is concerned with the total orientation of the self as a psycho-physical unity functioning in a way that is inconsistent with the will and purpose of God. And the word *spirit* (Greek *pneuma*) is associated with the self as a psycho-physical unity functioning in a way that is consistent with the will and purpose of God. Therefore, "while 'pneuma,' spirit, when it is used of man, is that in virtue of which he is open to and transmits the life of God (Rom. 8:16; cf. 1 Cor. 2:10f), 'sarx' is man in contrast with God."[10]

In an appraisal of the spiritual and spatial in traditional African religion, John S. Pobee makes it clear that the African world view is inclusive. We must recognize, however, as Pobee points out, that Africa is diverse, having over eight hundred languages, different cultures, and a variety of ecological conditions. While on the one hand I recognize the great danger involved in generalizing about the second largest continent in the world, on the other hand I support Pobee's assessment that the predominant perspective in the African world view is an integration of reality.[11]

Pobee's study involves an analysis of the Akan society. The Akan community is composed of such social groups as the Asante; the Bono, also referred to as the Brongs; Tui groups known as the Akwapim, Akim, and Akwammu; the Fante; the Denkyira; and the Wassaw. In spite of such diversity, Pobee's point is that in the Akan society religion is an all-pervasive phenomenon. In all key events and stages of life — including birth, death, marriage, and puberty — the activities of social institutions are inextricably bound up with the religious dimensions.[12]

Laurenti Magesa in "Authentic African Spirituality" points out that in the African context it is not right for the church to be concerned exclusively with the eternal in its proclamation of the gospel. Life as experienced here and now in this physical and spiritual plane is an important dimension of salvation. "Surely needed, therefore," writes Magesa, "is an authentic Christian spiritual life relevant to present-day Africa."[13]

Magesa is referring to an interpretation of the Christian faith in which the spiritual and spatial dimensions are interlocking categories. Such an approach integrates all facets of existence, which means that social justice, peace, liberation, and reconciliation become interrelated with salvation. Christian eschatological hope must deal with the temporal order and seek to realize freedom from poverty, ignorance, disease, social inequities, exploitation of resources, and other forms of dehumanization.[14] John S. Mbiti in *African Religions and Philosophies* helps to clarify the inclusive dimension of African religion that Magesa views as compatible with authentic Christian roots. Mbiti says:

> Because traditional religions permeate all the departments of life, there is no formal distinction between the sacred and the spiritual and the material areas of life. Wherever the African is, there is his or her religion: he carries it to the fields where he is sowing seeds or harvesting a crop; he takes it with him to the beer party or to attend a funeral ceremony; or if he is educated it is taken to the examination room at school or in the university; if he is a politician he takes it to the house of parliament.[15]

The point that Mbiti is making is that although the belief in life after death has a significant place in African societies, the quality of life experienced here and now is the primary concern in African religions. He contends that there is little, if any, focus on the distinctly spiritual dimension apart from the physical dimension. "No line is drawn between the spiritual and the physical."[16]

The orientation toward an integration of the spiritual and spatial, which characterizes the biblical tradition and African societies, is espoused in process metaphysics from beginning to end. It represents the direction that Christian theology must take, on a large scale, if we are to be serious about liberation. The dualistic approach fails to provide an inclusive approach to liberation. Whereas the inclusive approach contains liberating dimensions at every point.

A prevailing theme present in both Old and New Testament communities, for example, is the idea that eschatological hope consists of the promises of God and their fulfillment. It means that the present circumstances of humankind can never exhaust the magnitude of God's promises in history, for at any given moment in history God's promises are greater than humanity's capacity to exhaust those promises. This makes the present and the not-yet characteristic of the eschatological pilgrimage of the faith community. Even when individuals and groups have continuing peak experiences, it does not mean that eschatological hope is consummated. It does mean that the redemptive power of God is being partly realized in history; it means that the present and the not-yet dimensions of God's reign are becoming partially real in the world. The fulfillment of God's promises, therefore, is not to be perceived as a complete, once-and-for-all occurrence. It is dynamic and always in the process of becoming.

The liberating dimension to this is the recognition that these promises always contain both spiritual and spatial dimensions. The great error in Plato's world view, which was later assimilated into Christian theology, was the disjunction of the spiritual realm and the physical realm. When assimilated into Christian theology, the Platonic perspective steered Christian eschatological hope in the direction of otherworldliness; the goal of life was for the soul to escape from the body and return to its state of perfection in the heavens.

Whitehead's corrective to Plato brings these two realms into interrelatedness. Whitehead replaced Plato's "ideas" or "forms" with eternal objects. God's function in the primordial nature, as the reservoir of potentiality or possibility, is consistent with God's promises in the biblical tradition. These possibilities in God's primordial nature represent the highest aims or goals for humanity. The liberating aspect suggests that God's highest possibilities are always available to the human condition. This means that the options available to each person in history are far greater than all the limitations and restrictions that may be imposed upon that person by social structures.

Whitehead's integration of the spiritual and spatial dimensions gives to these options a socioeconomic, political context. This suggests that the salvific aspect of God's presence in history is the demand for social, economic, and political justice. We cannot make the disjunction between the spiritual and spatial that is made in Platonic thought. These dimensions must be perceived as interrelated in order for liberation to possess inclusiveness. Therefore, the transformation of the present involves the redemption of the whole person, including the physical, spiritual, and emotional dimensions. This is crucial for the liberation of the oppressed.

Viewing the self as a psycho-physical unity grounded in social relatedness implies that the transformation of the temporal realm must involve making a radical change in the social, economic, and political conditions that perpetuate oppression. The fact that many oppressed persons suffer increasingly from starvation, homelessness, inadequate medical care, and political colonialism, among a host of other social ills, provokes the urgent need to radically transform the conditions in the social order that continue to cause their suffering. This type of eschatological hope that relates to the existential needs of the oppressed makes a significant difference. Because the dualistic perspective puts too much emphasis on the spiritual realm, it lacks the degree of passion and commitment to the dynamic and pluralistic dimensions of existence necessary to inspire the transformation of societal structures. Dualism tends, on the contrary, to reinforce the status quo social philosophy.

When we place too much emphasis on the spiritual realm and not enough on the need to transform the present, we take a gradualistic approach to social change. And the philosophy of gradualism tends to focus more on perpetuating existing social systems in their present form, making only occasional minor modifications. It fails to involve dismantling the social systems that have proved to be inadequate and obsolete. It tends to resist the need to devise new models that are better able to attain human fulfillment. Martin Luther King, Jr., himself recognized the limitations present in the dualistic perspective and felt that it encouraged gradualism.[17]

This dualism, as I have sought to point out, has undergirded oppression in America and throughout the global village. We have yet to take to heart the words of Martin Luther King, Jr., which lift up inclusiveness and expose the inadequacy of a dualistic approach:

"Injustice anywhere is a threat to justice everywhere. We are caught in an inescapable network of mutuality, tied in a single garment of destiny. Whatever affects one directly, affects all indirectly."[18]

The Viability of Persuasive Ethical Theism for Liberating the Oppressed

Our task now is to identify ways in which divine persuasion offers liberating possibilities for victims of systemic oppression. To accomplish this we will need to clarify God's role and function in the liberation struggle in relation to humanity's role and function. As we attempt to do this it will be necessary at points to mention ways in which the traditional notion of God's omnipotence are not conducive to human liberation. My argument is that divine persuasion is viable for liberation because it maximizes human freedom. And divine omnipotence is not viable because it violates human freedom.

The gulf between God the world established by traditional theists and supernaturalists not only prevented God's participation in dynamic, pluralistic experiences in the world but also resulted in a definition of God's power that does not allow for genuine human freedom. Whitehead alludes to this when he points out that in traditional theism God is exempt from all the metaphysical categories that apply to humanity. This means that God was believed to be eminently real, which made all experiences in history derivatively real. Such a position makes God necessary to the world; but the world is not necessary to God. The gulf between God and the world led to what Whitehead refers to as "unqualified omnipotence." "The worst of unqualified omnipotence," says Whitehead, "is that it is accompanied by responsibility for every detail of every happening."[19]

Such an imbalance of power between God and the world makes God the supreme agency of compulsion, and that results in a wholly derivative world.[20] The consequence is that God becomes responsible for evil in the world. Whitehead argues that if such a position is adhered to, there is no explanation for evil other than ascribing its origin to God. Since God in traditional theism is responsible for all events in history, the origin of both good and evil must be ascribed to God. God "is then the supreme author of the play, and to Him must therefore be ascribed its shortcomings as well as its success," Whitehead says.[21]

Whitehead contends that ascribing all power to God in the sense that the world becomes merely derivative makes God into a tyrant, a despot, or a dictator.[22] Paul Tillich is critical of traditional theism for similar reasons. Tillich shares Whitehead's notion that within the framework of traditional theism human freedom is not possible. Tillich argues that the God of traditional theism is bound to the subject-object mode of thinking. God becomes an object for persons as subjects, and at the same time persons become objects for God as a subject. Consequently, God deprives persons of subjectivity because God is all-powerful and all-knowing. God becomes, according to Tillich, the invincible tyrant who violates the freedom and subjectivity of all persons.[23]

Whitehead and Tillich agree that in order to attain an understanding of human freedom that is consistent metaphysically with the nature of God, the traditional idea of omnipotence needs reconstructing. For victims of systemic oppression, the idea of an all-powerful God who is responsible for all events in the world works against liberation. And the notion that the future is guaranteed to be victorious for the oppressed because God is in control of history minimizes the urgent need for oppressed persons to commit themselves to attaining freedom.[24]

Such a goal requires the profound commitment of oppressed persons alongside God's sustaining spiritual resources. Frederick Douglass in his influential statement of 1849 "No Progress without Struggle" speaks to the need for oppressed persons to maximize their efforts toward attaining freedom. He says,

Let me give you a word of the philosophy of reforms. The whole history of the progress of human liberty shows that all concessions, yet made to her august claims, have been born of earnest struggle. The conflict has been exciting, agitating, all-absorbing, and for the time being putting all other tumults to silence. It must do this or it does nothing. If there is no struggle, there is no progress. Those who profess to favor freedom, and yet depreciate agitation, are men who want crops without plowing up the ground. They want rain without thunder and lightning. They want the ocean without the awful roar of its many waters. This struggle may be a moral one; or it may be a physical one; or it may be both moral and physical; but it must be a struggle.[25]

The idea of divine persuasion points us in the direction of arising to the task that Douglass suggests. Our efforts must be based on a partnership between God and humanity.

God's Persuasive Power

The nature of God's power is defined in process metaphysics as persuasive. In other words, God does not *choose* to be persuasive rather than coercive. God's being *is* persuasive. Whitehead applauds Plato for thus envisioning God's power. He was convinced that Plato's discovery that God's power is persuasive and not coercive was one of the greatest intellectual discoveries in the history of religion.[26] Since God's power is defined as persuasive, it then follows that God's role and function in the world are also persuasive. In this regard Whitehead says, "God's role is not the combat of productive force with productive force, or destructive force with destructive force."[27] For example, we can see God's persuasive power operative in history as oppressed minority social groups continue to appeal to the moral conscience of oppressors. Voices of protest against and discontent with forms of social injustice represent illustrations of God's persuasive power. We can see this taking place in South Africa among black South Africans; but it is also happening throughout Latin America, Asia, and North America itself. The voices of women in their quest for equal rights, American Indians in their quest to regain their land, Afro-Americans, Mexican Americans, Hispanics, and other social groups in their quest for economic development, all represent voices of God's persuasive power in history. God's persuasive power does not perpetuate the status quo. It challenges the status quo and calls for righteousness, justice, mercy, goodness, equality, and liberation. God's persuasive power never ceases in history. It always illumines new dimensions of what it means to be human. Wherever there is any form of oppression, God's persuasive power functions in a "prophetic" manner, discomforting the oppressor. It does not condone systemic evil; nor does it exonerate the oppressor. It radically calls for a dismantling of all oppressive forces in history.

Whereas God's persuasive power is a viable basis for human liberation, there are some essential factors that need to be considered when that power is elevated to an ethical theism. First we need to consider Whitehead's tendency to limit God's options in regard to power solely to persuasion. As I have said earlier, in Whitehead's process theism God's very nature is defined as persuasive. Although Lewis S. Ford has argued convincingly that the persuasive power of God is compatible with biblical theism, we cannot disregard the coercive elements of God's power that are also present in biblical theism. While I think it is true that persuasive power is more conducive to human freedom, I also know, speaking realistically, that some degrees of coercion are built within the creative process itself. This is not to suggest that we should develop an ethical theism based on coercion. Rather, we should recognize that coercion is a phenomenon built within the fabric of the creative process, alongside persuasion.

Now in what sense is coercion built into the creative process? A naturalistic approach to suffering suggests that things in the world to a degree are mutually obstructive, meaning that they possess inherent tendencies toward perishing. This aspect of reality may be prolonged, slowed down, or prevented temporarily, but it cannot be eliminated from the natural process. It comes as a form of coercion. Death is the obvious and ultimate example.

We also experience forms of coercion in the world of nonhuman nature. In hurricanes, drought, tornadoes, and earthquakes, natural process takes on a self-destructive dimension. Although destructive to many life forms of the natural environment as well as to humans, that unavoidable process is essential to the sustaining vitality of nature. It means that things are constantly being born in the natural environment and things are constantly perishing.

God's role in all this is not to inflict pain and suffering through coercion. It is not to combat physical force with physical force. It is not to coerce humanity and the world into conformity with a prescribed plan. Rather, God's role is to persuade humanity toward the self-actualization of its highest possibilities.

I also realize, however, that it is not possible to develop any philosophical, theological, or ethical system that is entirely compatible with the wide range of options contained in the Bible. The Bible was not written as a systematic document. Therefore, rather than to use the Bible as the source for precept and example, our task is to use it as the basic source of theology, thereby allowing insights gained from the Bible, experience, tradition, revelation, church history, and reason to enter into the formulation of an ethical theism that is conducive to human liberation.

The viability of persuasion as an ethical theism that can eradicate oppression depends upon the extent to which the majority social group is willing to move toward redistributing wealth, power, and control of resources. Obviously this cannot be achieved without facing the inevitable conflict and tension provoked by change and hostility. By putting emphasis on negating and condemning the efforts of the oppressed to protest the whims of power structures, the majority condemns their efforts and makes the victims of oppression appear to be the perpetrators of violence. Too infrequently does the majority social group emphasize the psychological, social, political, economic, and cultural violence it often imposes upon minority social groups. This attitude blocks the power of persuasive ethical theism from eradicating oppression.

Frederick Douglass was surely correct in recognizing that "power concedes nothing without demand. It never has and never will." Here emerges the crucial factor that challenges the viability of persuasive ethical theism to eradicate oppression. Have the problems of sexism, racism, classism, and imperialism become so entrenched in social structures that the majority social group is not willing to concede? To what extent, for example, is the oppressive government of South Africa willing to concede? And will the majority social group concede with sufficient urgency to satisfy the growing thirst for freedom of the oppressed? Will ethical gradualism satisfy this thirst? Or will this thirst take a form of radicalism that is informed by persuasive ethical theism?

What we usually find in institutionalized systems of oppression is that the controlling majority social group tends to allow economic gain to take precedence over its moral conscience. This is why power does not concede without demand. The modern institution of slavery, for example, was built upon an economic system of cheap labor. It took the Civil War to dismantle the machinery of slavery. It took persuasive ethical theism in the form of nonviolent direct action to put an end to the institutionalization of second-class citizenship for Afro-Americans.

During the earliest stage of the Civil Rights struggle we did not succeed in desegregating public accommodations, including segregated buses, until boycotts of public transportation and other public facilities greatly affected the economy. I am not suggesting, however, that we should use the same strategies today in dealing with present social ills. We must always seek new models of social change based on prevailing social conditions. But what I am pointing out is that economic factors usually stand in the way of our ability to become totally open and vulnerable to the will of God.

The Divine-human Partnership for Social Change

The role and function of God's persuasive power can be seen more fully in what Whitehead describes as the principle of concretion. I mentioned earlier that one function of God's primordial nature is to serve as the ground or source of all potentiality in the world.[28] God's role as the principle of concretion means that God directs or orders the ingression of all possibilities into the world. Although Whitehead also uses principles of limitation[29] and determination[30] in describing God, the principle of concretion is more generic. God directs possibilities into the world through persuasion, not coercion. In this way God is the source of order in the world. In other words, without God's role in setting some boundaries to emerging possibilities in the world through persuasive influence, the world would end up in anarchy.

The liberating dimension in God's persuasive power comes in when each social group recognizes that it has the responsibility of claiming its freedom in society. God aids the liberation process through the constant flow of inexhaustible possibilities into the world. This is an act of grace on God's part. The transformation and liberation of the human condition cannot take place apart from the participation of God and individuals in social action. God's role is not to violate human freedom in the quest for liberation. Victims of systemic oppression must claim freedom by maximizing efforts toward social transformation. The significant point here is that God does not violate the inherent freedom of each individual. God does not impose possibilities on individuals. Rather, God initiates a conglomeration of ideal possibilities for individuals. The decision to accept or reject these possibilities resides solely within the individual. It is through persuasive influence that God protects the inherent freedom of individuals. When they claim their inherent freedom by transforming inhuman conditions in society, the creative partnership between God and humanity functions toward liberation.

God and humanity become agents of social change. The purpose of social change is to help individuals realize their inherent freedom. In God's consequent nature God is interwoven with social change. God is not removed from it. In God's primordial nature God is permanent, but in God's consequent nature God is constantly participating in the changing processes of existence. God is affected by these changes. And God in like manner affects individuals in the world. God uses all available resources to help them realize their goals. Their self-realization is an instance of conditioned freedom.[31]

Conditioned freedom means that there are boundaries placed on freedom. But these boundaries are not deterministic, as in the Newtonian mechanistic perspective. Neither are they predeterministic as is found in Hegelian dialectical pantheism. Rather, they are indeterministic. In the philosophy of determinism the future is predictable based on past and present experiences. I tried to show earlier how determinism was used in the context of traditional theism to sustain the marginal existence of Afro-Americans, women, American Indians, and others. Determinism perpetuates the status quo and leaves no hope for oppressed persons to bring about a fundamental change in their predicament. And predeterminism has the same unhappy consequences for oppressed persons because it justified all events in history based on the notion that they are manifestations of God's cosmic plan.

The Suffering God and the Oppressed: Critical Reflections on Ethical Implications

The challenge facing us now is to reflect critically upon Whitehead's process theodicy, seeking to determine its relevance for victims of systemic oppression. This requires us to consider some ethical implications. The reality of evil is a major problem for humanity in general and oppressed social groups in particular. In addition to facing the evils inherent in the evolutionary process, oppressed social groups have to cope with the malfunctions caused by systemic inequities. In what way does Whitehead's process theodicy address these problems? In order for process metaphysics to maintain viability for constructing a model of cultural pluralism, its response to theodicy must be tested against the reality of systemic oppression.

Theodicy is perhaps theology's most difficult challenge. Charles Hartshorne defines the challenge succinctly: "The most serious problem confronting the organic analogy, if not all theological conceptions, is that of evil. How can there be conflict, disorder, defects, in the body of God; or, if there are none, what are we to make of empirical evils and of our feeling that we should try to mitigate these?"[32]

Although Whitehead makes a concentrated effort to resolve the problem of theodicy in metaphysics,[33] when it comes to translating his philosophical program into an ethical theory that offers possibilities for human liberation, there is a need to extrapolate from Whitehead's basics in raising some fundamental issues about theodicy.

Whitehead and the Problem of Loss

Whitehead provides the image of God's participation in the world as "the fellow sufferer who understands."[34] God loses nothing in the world that can be saved. God's consequent nature functions here somewhat like the idea of the eternal now. By that I mean God's consequent nature always coexists with the world. This happens everlastingly. As a nonperishing actual entity participating in the perishing flux of creaturely existence, God influences every actuality in the world toward the attainment of its highest possibilities. In the process of doing this God also shares in the sufferings, sorrows, failures, victories, and joys of the world. God is forever present existentially and is always intimately related to every creature. Even the revolts of destructive evil, which Whitehead considers self-regarding — the good they achieved was in individual joy and individual sorrow — are saved by God. "The image under which this operative growth of God's nature is best conceived, is that of a tender care that nothing be lost," says Whitehead.[35]

Whitehead believes that the fundamental religious problem is related to the problem of loss or perishing. The fact of the matter is that things perish; perishing is inevitable. "The ultimate evil in the temporal world," says Whitehead, "is deeper than any specific evil. It lies in the fact that the past fades, that time is a perpetual perishing."[36] Humanity searches for novelty in face of the terror of the loss of the past. Human beings have great difficulty accepting loss and dealing effectively with the reality of transitoriness, and Whitehead considers this to be the fundamental religious problem. The extreme aspect of this problem constitutes the existential reality of death.

Whitehead's integration of temporality and everlastingness is an effort to answer the religious questions related to transitoriness, death, perishing, and the loss of the past. This loss of the past has to do with what Whitehead calls "subjective immediacy." By subjective immediacy he means the internal activity or vitality of actual occasions. Each actual occasion is an experiencing subject and needs internal vitality to reach self-actualization. "This self-functioning is the real internal constitution of an actual entity."[37] Whitehead's resolution to the fundamental religious problem is that after each experiencing subject perishes its immediacy becomes integrated into God's consequent nature everlastingly.

This is to say that after each experiencing subject reaches self-actualization, it perishes and becomes an integral part of God's being. Whitehead calls this objective *immortality*. Upon perishing subjects become data that are used by God in history to influence future subjects toward self-actualization. In this way God loses nothing in the world that can be saved. Once subjects become incarnated into God's consequent nature, there is no loss; neither is there any obstruction of past occasions. God is always immediately related to all past occasions. Whitehead's effort is to combine the creative advance of the world with the retention of mutual immediacy. He integrates everlastingness into temporality. "In everlastingness, immediacy is reconciled with objective immortality."[38]

As opposed to making an ultimate disjunction between temporality and spatiality in the quest of a mystified state of everlastingness in heaven beyond history, as in the Platonic tradition, Whitehead suggests that after experiencing subjects become actualized, they are transformed and perfected in God, and through God they flow back into the temporal world. Each emerging new actual occasion experiences this actualized data as relevant for its self-actualization. This makes the kingdom of heaven existentialized within history in a dynamic manner. There is a reciprocal relation between temporality and eternality. "What is done in the world is transformed into a reality in heaven, and the reality in heaven passes back into the world."[39]

The consequent nature of God is God's judgment upon the world. God saves the world by retaining the best of each creature into God's nature. Not only does God use the best of actual occasions, but God also "uses what in the temporal world is mere wreckage."[40] The idea advanced here is that when God's love flows back into the world, it amounts to the transmutation of present evil into some sense of positive good. This is done in the consequent nature of God in that God possesses the ideal vision for each actual evil and meets it with a novel result, which restores goodness into the world.[41]

For Whitehead God has in the divine nature the knowledge of evil, pain, and degradation, but it is overcome with what is good. The facts of creaturely experiences, whether they consist of pleasure, joy, or pain, are "woven immortally into the rhythm of mortal things. Its very evil becomes a stepping stone in the all-embracing ideas of God."[42]

Let us now turn our attention to ascertaining the relevance of Whitehead's response to evil to victims of systemic oppression.

The Origin of Evil

First of all, we must consider the process by which evil originates in the world. Whitehead feels that he has responded to this concern sufficiently by resorting to the persuasive power of God. Since actual occasions are self-creative in the sense that God's role is to initiate the highest possibilities and not to coerce actual occasions into conformity with these possibilities, it follows that God is not responsible for the decisions made by actual occasions in the world, including humanity. However, in the self-actualization process, which emerging possibilities experience as they make a transition from potentiality to actuality, God participates fully in the concrescence of experience in the world.

Does this mean, therefore, that God participates in the evil as well as the good? In Whitehead's theodicy God does not discriminate in choosing which particular experiences to participate in. In other words, God does not select from the wide range of experiences in the world to become involved with some and not to be involved with others. If God participates in the concrescence of actual occasions that are perceived by the human community as evil, does this mean that God participates in evil? Let us list some examples: sexism, racism, classism, imperialism, the apartheid system in South Africa, the Holocaust, slavery, segregation, terrorism, nuclear annihilation. Does God participate in such evils? In Whitehead's idea of the concrescence of actual occasions, which includes a process geared toward the realization of aims, goals, value, and purpose, does he not leave himself open to the charge that tragedy, loss, and obstruction are the cost of the evolutionary process itself? Such a position would result in a resignation to the present social order. And if this is the case, are we to extrapolate from the human condition that problems related to tragedy, loss, and obstruction will eventually work themselves out as they do in the natural order? For White-head God does not reject the negative aspects of evolution. Rather, God harmonizes the negative aspects of evolution into God's conse-quent nature and integrates them into the unity of God's experience in the world. It seems that in Whitehead's system God has resolved the problem of evil within God's nature. But what about systemic suffering in society? What implication does God's resolution of evil have for oppressed persons?

Can Rationality Alone Bring Liberation?

It seems to me that Whitehead embraces such profound optimism about the inherent power of rationality to overcome human alien-ation and suffering in the world that he disregards the need for God's transforming power to eradicate sin. But in addition to the transforming power of God through grace functioning alongside human reason in assisting humanity toward fulfillment, what other role does God perform in transforming the self? Apart from keep-ing the highest possibilities before humanity, which represent those past actual occasions that have been redeemed by God to be used everlastingly in influencing history, does God possess the concrete power to transform the sinfulness of humanity? And although God's cosmic rationality resolves the problem of evil within God's own na-ture, how does God's rationality make a difference to the oppressed in overcoming marginal existence?

Does God's provision of the highest possibilities to the oppressed and the oppressor through rationality amount to any more than a growing sensitivity of God to human oppression and a mere deep-ening of God's role as an empathetic listener? My point here is to urge us to be skeptical of the inherent capacity of rationality alone to overcome systemic oppression. I urge such skepticism because mod-ern consciousness has been conditioned to acquiesce to the majority social group's need to control and monopolize human and natural resources, and hence the goals and purposes of rationality — espe-cially that of the majority social group — have become distorted.

We have learned to esteem leisure and wealth as ultimate values and thus have greatly impaired the capacity of the majority social group to employ rationality alone in eradicating systemic oppression. And the increasingly audible groans of the oppressed have yet to persuade the oppressors that it is in their best interest to set the captives free.

Process theodicy does not posit a God who will unilaterally take charge of history and eradicate oppressive forces. Whitehead makes the point that God's role is not to create the world, but to save it through "tender patience leading it by his vision of truth, beauty and goodness." God's role, as Whitehead puts it, is not to counteract force with force, whether the situation is positive or negative. God's role is to lose nothing that can be saved, possess tender love and care for the world, maintain infinite patience in humanity, and keep before fallen humanity a degree of the overpowering rationality of God's conceptual harmonization.

Does this mean that oppressed persons are to wait patiently while God appeals to oppressive forces through rationality? To do this, as I have said earlier, would result in a kind of ethical quietism and a status quo social philosophy. The strength of Whitehead's theodicy is its affirmation that the human condition, regardless of its degree of alienation and oppression, can never become hopeless, because God's patience is infinite. But because of human finite patience and weaknesses, we cannot construe God's infinite patience as dictating an ethic of gradualism for effecting social change.

Ethical gradualism leads to complacency, apathy, paternalism, and indifference. Oppressed persons' current demands for freedom and social justice suggest the need for us to develop a critical interpretation of God's infinite patience. The time to overcome oppression is now. We cannot procrastinate. We must move toward the realization of social justice with urgency.

It is true that because God will never lose faith in the human condition, we should not lose faith in each other. It is also true that the growing gulf between the rich and the poor, if not dealt with now, could result in the destruction of both the oppressed and the oppressors. The future can be a threat or it can be an opportunity.

There is no guarantee of a victorious future where the oppressed and oppressor are liberated. God will not take charge of history unilaterally and enforce a victorious future. It is up to the oppressed and oppressors, as they continue to experience God's transforming grace, to determine together what the future will be. The future is open. It is not closed.

While it is true for Whitehead that God participates in the concrescence of each emerging actual occasion, Whitehead argues contrary to the notion that all actual occasions conform to the nature of God. Based on the idea of God's inclusiveness it is essential for God to be taken into account in every phase of the creative process. Without this the boundless wealth of possibility would have no order. The inclusion of an ordered balance in the world requires the continued presence of an actual entity in the world possessing "its own unchanged consistency of character on every phase."[43] The unchanged consistency of God means that although God participates in change, God's nature has no evil or negative aspects. In this regard, Whitehead says,

> Thus if God be an actual entity which enters into every creative phase and yet is above change, He must be exempt from internal inconsistency which is the note of evil. Since God is actual, He must include in himself a synthesis of the total universe. There is, therefore, in God's nature the aspect of the realm of forms as qualified by the world, and the aspect of the world as qualified by the forms. His completion, so that He is exempt from transition into something else, must mean that his nature remains self-consistent in relation to all change.[44]

Although there is truth in the notion that the evolutionary process contains manifestations of tragedy, loss, and obstruction, we have to be careful not to use this to justify the inequities and imbalances afflicting minority social groups. These social problems result from human greed and a need to feel superior. They represent evils that humanity imposes on the natural order. While I realize that this historical process itself — including values, traditions, aesthetics, and morals — is something humanity imposes on the natural order, my point is that in examining the problem of evil in the human community, we must look beyond the response of the evolutionary process to natural evils.

For example, Whitehead says, "Thus evil promotes its own elimination by destruction, or degradation, or by elevation."[45] He contends that evil exhibited in physical and mental suffering consists of the loss of the higher experience in favor of the lower experience. In its own nature evil is unstable.[46] It is my strong conviction that majority and minority social groups must feel a great urgency to oppose evil forces in society and work toward their elimination. We cannot expect institutional racism and sexism, for instance, to eliminate themselves. We have to develop social and institutional strategies designed to overcome them. This raises another question.

How does Whitehead's idea of God's initiation and conservation of value in history make a significant difference to social ills in history? And how does the value that is objectified and retained everlastingly in God's memory offer redemptive possibilities to social ills?

Learning from the Past

Value, for Whitehead, is inherent within actuality itself. To be an actual entity in the world means to possess self-identity, self-creation, and self-interest. It seems that underlying Whitehead's scheme is the idea that because God retains value in the world through a memory process, and because this value participates in history in an ongoing manner, it provides the context for redemption. His thinking suggests that because God's primordial nature initiates value in the world and God's consequent nature conserves this value once it becomes realized in history, value becomes redemptive for future actual occasions. Emerging future occasions are influenced by the value retained in God's consequent nature as they seek self-actualization. Whitehead's proposal makes the past that is retained everlastingly in God crucial in persuading humanity to live responsibly in the present.

It seems to me that the redemptive possibilities contained in God open up liberating possibilities for human existence only when we allow them to make a significant difference in influencing the decisions we make in the present. The extent to which we really learn and grow from the past determines the extent to which the possibilities retained in God have the capacity to affect history. For if we fail to learn from our past failures and successes, the redemptive power of God will become very limited. In fact, we could say that our knowledge of the past, as it is retained in God everlastingly, is sufficient to offer liberating possibilities to the present only if we are sufficiently open to it. Whitehead refers to this when he says, "Each tragedy is the disclosure of an ideal: — What might have been, and was not: What can be. The tragedy was not in vain. This survival power in motive force, by reason of appeal to reserves of Beauty, marks the difference between the tragic evil and the gross evil."[47]

For example, modern humanity should have learned from the Holocaust in Germany during World War II that anti-Semitism is wrong. But in spite of our knowledge of the past, anti-Semitism persists. What have we learned from the American institution of slavery? Many declare that the Holocaust and slavery could never occur again. But when we witness the injustice of the South African apartheid system, for instance, and the increasing conflicts between superpowers and emerging Third World powers, we begin to feel that the evils of the past are not as distant from the present as some might think. The human condition impedes the liberating and salvific possibilities contained in God's redemption when it fails to integrate lessons from past mistakes into present actions.

Before God's conservation of value in history can become redemptive for human existence, majority and minority social groups have to stand together in opposition to social injustice. This is required for true cultural pluralism to be realized. But this also requires the majority social group to change its behavior, a change that takes place when humanity responds positively to God's redemption. The majority cannot continue to exploit the minorities and feel that God's conservation of value through memory of the past makes a significant difference to our present predicament. God's creative redemptive power takes place in history when, on the basis of learning from past successes, failures, joys, and sorrows, we make decisions in the present that aim toward a more equitable and just society. Those at the top of the socioeconomic ladder must begin to listen earnestly enough to the concerns of marginalized persons that they will be moved to creative action. Jürgen Moltmann ably puts it in these words: "Thus one has to listen to them and one has to let them talk, if one wants to get to know the real conditions of the present and wants to understand that future for which it pays to hope."[48] To listen this way means to be open to these oppressed groups, to become sensitive to their problems. Creative listening and social action are interrelated. Both groups can then lay claim to the processes of change, acting interdependently. This differs from the philosophy of integration we experienced in the 1960s.

During that time Afro-Americans, for example, were never made an integral part of the decision-making process. Because they were not allowed to participate in every significant decision that affected their lives, though they experienced public integration of restaurants, hotels, schools, hospitals, churches, and other facilities, they ended up with a feeling of powerlessness. Afro-Americans were not able to escape economic dependency and move toward acquiring interdependence with the power structure. The key to freedom and liberation is enabling oppressed minority social groups to take charge of their own lives. This process is called *empowerment*.

Freedom involves establishing interdependent social relations. The extent to which the majority social group is willing to participate in the empowerment of minority social groups and the extent to which minority social groups are allowed to share interdependently in decision-making processes will determine the success or failure of efforts to achieve liberation for all of humanity.

This interdependence also applies to one oppressed social group's relationship to another. It is true that each oppressed social group is unique, but a sense of interrelatedness should help us to find unity in diversity. This is not advocating a monocentric system that would dissolve our differences. To the contrary, interrelatedness helps each group affirm its efforts individually while at the same time becoming an integral part of other groups. We must seek to maintain both individual and corporate aspects of God's redemptive possibilities in history.

We cannot afford to work for freedom as adversaries. We must discover new methods of negotiation and collaboration and integrate those into creative strategies for social change. Strategies that are grounded in a vision of reality as interrelated broadcast the truth that whatever affects any particular social group in any part of the global village affects all the rest of humanity indirectly. Martin Luther King, Jr., was right when he said, "Together we must learn to live as brothers and sisters or together we will be forced to perish as fools."[49]

Notes

Chapter 1

1. Marjorie P. K. Weiser, ed., *Ethnic America* (New York: H. W. Wilson Co., 1978), 4.

2. J. Milton Yinger, "Social Forces Involved in Group Identification or Withdrawal," *Daedalus* (Spring 1961): 247–62.

3. The idea of "Anglo conformity" was used originally by Steward and Mildred Cole. See Steward G. Cole and Mildred Wiese Cole, *Minorities and the American Promise* (New York: Harper and Brothers, 1954), 160. Milton M. Gordon points out that "Anglo conformity" has been the prevailing ideology of assimilation goals operative throughout American history. See Milton M. Gordon, "Assimilation in America: Theory and Reality," *Daedalus* 90 (Spring): 247–85. Gordon's discussion is based on a larger study that he completed for the Russell Stage Foundation; that study was later published under the title *Assimilation in American Life* (New York: Oxford University Press, 1964). Also, see James Stuart Olson, *The Ethnic Dimension in American History* (New York: St. Martin's Press, 1979), xv–xxv.

4. See Oscar Handlin, "Historical Perspectives on the American Ethnic Group," *Daedalus* (Spring 1961): 220–32; L. Paul Metzger, "American Sociology and Black Assimilation: Conflicting Perspectives," *American Journal of Sociology* 76:627–47.

5. Quoted from Sidney E. Ahlstrom, *A Religious History of the American People* (New Haven: Yale University Press, 1972), 515.

6. W. E. B. Du Bois, *The Souls of Black Folk* (New York: Fawcett Pub., 1968), 17.

7. Ibid.

8. Ibid., 15–22.

9. William M. Newman, *American Pluralism* (New York: Harper and Row, 1973), 9.

10. Ibid., 56.

11. Ibid. For an acute perspective on the immigration process, see Marcus Lee Hanson, *The Atlantic Migration: 1607-1840* (Cambridge, Mass.: Harvard University Press, 1940).

12. Hanson, *The Atlantic Migration*, 54-60.

13. Ibid., 56-66.

14. "Invasion-succession," a sociological category, denotes how members of the white community move out as members of minority social groups begin to move in.

15. See Gordon, *Assimilation in American Life*, 115-31. Other discussions of the "melting pot" theory can be found in John Higham, *Strangers in the Land* (New Brunswick, N.J.: Rutgers University Press, 1955); Philip Gleason, "The Melting Pot: Symbol of Fusion or Confusion?" *American Quarterly* 16 (Spring 1964): 20-46; Oscar Handlin, *Immigration as a Factor in American History* (Englewood Cliffs, N.J.: Prentice Hall, 1959); *The American School and the Melting Pot*, ed. Natalie Isser and Lita Linzer Schwart (Bristol, Ind.: Wyndham Hall Press, 1985).

16. William Peterson, Michael Novak, and Philip Gleason, eds., *Concepts of Ethnicity* (Cambridge, Mass.: Harvard University Press, 1980), 80-84. Also see Gordon, *Assimilation in American Life*, 115-18.

17. See Gordon, *Assimilation in American Life*, 116. See also Israel Zangwill, *The Melting Pot* (New York: Macmillan Co., 1909), 37-199.

18. See Frederick Jackson Turner, *The Frontier in American History* (New York: Henry Holt and Co., 1920); Gordon, *Assimilation in American Life*, 115-20. For a critical appraisal of Turner's thesis, see George Rogers Taylor, ed., *The Turner Thesis Concerning the Role of the Frontier in American History* (Boston: D. C. Heath and Co., 1947).

19. Newman, *American Pluralism*, 61; see Madison Grant, *The Passing of the Great Race* (New York: Charles Scribner's Sons, 1916). For an authoritative source dealing with the development of race, see Thomas F. Gossett, *Race: The History of an Idea in America* (Dallas: Southern Methodist University Press, 1963).

20. W. E. B. Du Bois, *The World and Africa* (New York: International Publishers, 1947).

21. Newman, *American Pluralism*, 61.

22. Gordon, *Assimilation in American Life*, 116; see also Oscar Handlin's discussion in *Immigration as a Factor in American History*, 146.

23. Quoted in Handlin, *Immigration as a Factor in American History*, 120-21.

24. James A. Banks, "Teaching Ethnic Studies: Key Issues and Concepts,"

in *New Perspectives on School Integration*, ed. Murray Friedman, Roger Meltzer, and Charles Miller (Philadelphia: Fortress Press, 1979), 48–63. Banks shows sensitivity to the unique situation that pigmentation makes for Afro-Americans and other nonwhite ethnic minority social groups in the assimilation process. This is the reason why the new ethnic consciousness needs to be radically different from traditional approaches.

25. See William Greenbaum, "America in Search of a New Ideal: An Essay on the Rise of Pluralism," *Harvard Educational Review* 44/32 (August 1974): 414–440; Nathan Glazier and Daniel Moynihan, eds., *Ethnicity Theory and Experience* (Cambridge, Mass.: Harvard University Press, 1975); Henry J. Perkinson, "Education and the New Pluralism," *Review Journal of Philosophy and Social Science* 1/1 (1976): 1–14; Michael Novak, *The Rise of the Unmeltable Ethnics: Politics and Culture in the Seventies* (New York: Macmillan, 1973); A. M. Greeley, *Why Can't They Be Like Us? America's White Ethnic Groups* (New York: Institute of Human Relations Press, 1960); Peter Schrag, *The Decline of the W.A.S.P.* (New York: Morrow, 1940); Nicholas Appleton, *Cultural Pluralism in Education* (New York: Longman, 1983), 22.

26. Greenbaum, "America in Search of a New Ideal," 412–13.

27. Quoted from Weiser, *Ethnic America*, 4.

28. Novak, *Rise of the Unmeltable Ethnics*, 43–44.

29. Weiser, *Ethnic America*, 4.

30. See George Eaton Simpson and J. Milton Yinger, *Racial and Cultural Minorities* (New York: Harper and Row, 1965), 16. Another factor to be considered in defining majority-minority intergroup relations in America is the reality of economics. For example, in many urban areas Afro-Americans and Hispanics are the majority population, yet they remain at a low economic level. Even where these minorities are beginning to control the political process as local majorities, the economic situation of the masses still does not change significantly. This suggests that in the quest for cultural pluralism, economic factors must be taken seriously.

31. Newman, *American Pluralism*, 33.

32. One of Whitehead's pervasive critiques of the modern world view deals in its bifurcation of nature. It is this which Whitehead feels contributed to the domination of the environment, the exploitation and rape of the natural resources. See Alfred North Whitehead, *Concept of Nature* (New York: Cambridge University Press, 1978). See also William Ernest Hocking, "Whitehead on Mind and Nature," in *The Philosophy of Alfred North Whitehead*, ed. Paul Arthur Schilpp (Evanston, Il.: Northwestern University, 1941), 381–404.

33. George S. Brett, "Newton's Place in the History of Religious

Thought," in *Sir Isaac Newton: A Bicentenary Evaluation of His Work,* ed. The History of Science Society (London: Bailliere, Tindall and Cox, 1928), 263. For a comprehensive discussion of the Newtonians, see Margaret C. Jacob, *The Newtonians and the English Revolution, 1688–1720* (Ithaca, N.Y.: Cornell University Press, 1976).

34. See Thomas S. Kuhn, *The Structure of Scientific Revolutions* (Chicago: University of Chicago Press, 1970), 12.

35. Edwin Arthur Burtt, *The Metaphysical Foundations of Modern Physical Science* (New York: Harcourt, Brace and Co., 1927), 202–3.

36. Whitehead, *Science and the Modern World* (New York: Macmillan Co., 1925), 16.

37. David Tracy, *Blessed Rage for Order: The New Pluralism in Theology* (New York: The Seabury Press, 1978), 23. Tracy has done several penetrating studies on theological pluralism and contemporary culture. See David Tracy, *The Analogical Imagination: Christian Theology and the Culture of Pluralism* (New York: Crossroad, 1981).

38. Alfred North Whitehead, *Process and Reality* (New York: The Free Press, 1978), 7.

39. F. Bradford Wallack, *The Epochal Nature of Process in Whitehead's Process Metaphysics* (Albany: State University of New York, 1980), 2–3.

40. John Henry Randall, Jr., *The Making of the Modern Mind* (Boston: Houghton Mifflin Co., 1926), 524.

41. Ibid., 524.

42. Wallack, *Whitehead's Metaphysics,* 3. See also Whitehead, *Concept of Nature,* 70.

43. René Descartes, *Discourse on Method and Meditations* (New York: The Bobbs-Merrill Co., n.d.), 75–143.

44. George F. Thomas, *Religious Philosophies of the West* (New York: Charles Scribner's Sons, 1965), 176.

45. Descartes, *Discourse on Method,* 75–143.

46. Thomas, *Religious Philosophies,* 175–96.

47. Whitehead, *Science and the Modern World,* 58.

48. Ibid.

49. Randall, *Making of the Modern Mind,* 146.

50. Quoted from John Hope Franklin, *From Slavery to Freedom* (New York: Vintage Books, 1967), 43.

51. See ibid., 44.

52. Whitehead, *Science and the Modern World,* 72–79.

53. W. E. B. Du Bois, *The Souls of Black Folk,* 23.

54. W. E. B. Du Bois, *The World and Africa* (New York: International Publishers, 1965), 20.

55. The degree to which Afro-Americans lost their African cultural heritage upon enslavement in America has been an issue of long debate among scholars. For example, Melville F. Herskovits, Carter J. Woodson, and W. E. B. Du Bois have argued convincingly that African survivals were retained in Afro-American culture, including music, dance, religion, and arts. For a thorough discussion of African survivals in music see John Lovell, Jr., *Black Song: The Forge and The Flame* (New York: The Macmillan Co., 1972).

56. In Congress, 4 July 1776, The Unanimous Declaration of the Thirteen United States of America.

57. Quoted in Constance Baker Motley, "The Legal Status of the Negro in the United States," in *The American Negro Reference Book*, ed. John P. Davis (Englewood Cliffs, N.J.: Prentice Hall, n.d.), 485.

58. Quoted in ibid.

59. Ibid.

60. Paul Tillich, *Systematic Theology* (Chicago: The University of Chicago Press, 1963), 65.

61. Paul Tillich, *Theology of Culture* (London: Oxford University Press, 1959), 176.

62. Ibid.

63. Rem B. Edwards, *Reason and Religion* (New York: Harcourt Brace, 1972), 188–215.

64. Whitehead, *Process and Reality*, 343.

65. See Charles Hartshorne and William L. Reese, eds., *Philosophers Speak of God* (Chicago: University of Chicago Press, 1953), 1–25.

66. Edwards, *Reason and Religion*, 190.

67. Ibid.

68. Thomas, *Religious Philosophies*, 34–45.

69. Ibid.

70. Edwards, *Reason and Religion*, 189–93.

71. Martin Luther King, Jr., "Drum Major Instinct," in *Preaching the Gospel*, ed. Henry James Young (Philadelphia: Fortress Press, 1976), 41.

72. The idea that God is on the side of the oppressed is a prevailing theme throughout the classic literature of the Afro-American religious heritage. See Benjamin E. Mays, *The Negro's God* (New York: Atheneum, 1968); David Walker, "Walker's Appeal," in *The Ideological Origins of Black Nationalism*, ed. Sterling Stuckey (Boston: Beacon Press, 1972), 39–117; Clifton H. Johnson, ed., *God Struck Me Dead* (Boston: Pilgrim Press, 1969). For contemporary discussions, see works by James H. Cone, *God of the Oppressed*

(New York: Seabury Press, 1975); *A Black Theology of Liberation* (Philadelphia: Lippincott Co., 1970); and *Black Theology and Black Power* (New York: Seabury Press, 1969). Also, see works by J. Deotis Roberts, *Liberation and Reconciliation* (Philadelphia: Westminster Press, 1971); and *A Black Political Theology* (Philadelphia: Westminster Press, 1974).

73. Howard Thurman, *Deep River* (New York: Kennikat Press, 1969), 55–62.

74. For a discussion of the Hegelian school see William J. Brazill, *The Young Hegelians* (New Haven: Yale University Press, 1970); and Sidney Hook, *From Hegel to Marx* (Ann Arbor: University of Michigan Press, 1968).

75. Thomas, *Religious Philosophies*, 279–84.

76. Ibid., 280.

77. Ibid., 285.

78. Hook, *From Hegel to Marx*, 19–22.

79. Ibid.

80. Thomas, *Religious Philosophies*, 284–85.

81. G. W. F. Hegel, *The Philosophy of History*, trans. J. Sibree (New York: P. F. Collier and Son, 1902), 157. Hegel simply disregards the many significant contributions that black Africans have made to human culture and the development of civilization. For example, Lerone Bennett in *Before the Mayflower: A History of the Negro in America 1619–1964* (Chicago: Johnson Publishing Co., 1964) shows that civilization itself started in the great river valleys of Africa and Asia. Bennett indicates that people from Northern Africa "were among the first people to use tools, paint pictures, plant seeds and worship gods" (5). Following such eminent scholars as W. E. B. Du Bois, Carter G. Woodson, and William Leo Hansberry, Bennett holds that the ancient Egyptians, from Menes to Cleopatra, were a mixed race and exemplified the same type of physical features and color ranges as Afro-Americans. Carter G. Woodson is reputed to have said, "If the Egyptians and the majority of the tribes of Northern Africa were not Negroes, then, there are no Negroes in the United States" (7). See Carter G. Woodson, *African Background Outlined* (Washington, D.C.: n.pub., 1936); W. E. B. Du Bois, *Black Folk, Then and Now*; John Hope Franklin, *From Slavery to Freedom*.

82. Hegel, *Philosophy of History*, 157.

83. Ibid., 148–57.

84. Ibid., 153–57.

85. Ibid., 151.

86. Ibid., 150–57.

87. Ibid., 153.

88. The Hegelian system had a pervasive influence in Western civilization.

89. Newman, *American Pluralism*, 67.

90. Weiser, *Ethnic America*, 91–125.

91. Whitehead, *Adventures of Ideas* (New York: Macmillan, 1933), 354.

92. Ibid.

93. Ibid.

Chapter 2

1. Alfred North Whitehead, *Religion in the Making* (New York: The Macmillan Co., 1926), 84.

2. Whitehead, *Process and Reality* (New York: The Free Press, 1978), 3–13.

3. Ibid., 13.

4. Talcott Parsons, *The Social System* (New York: Free Press, 1964), 327.

5. Thomas S. Kuhn, *The Structure of Scientific Revolutions* (Chicago: University of Chicago Press, 1970), 52–91.

6. Park, *Race and Culture* (Glencoe, Il.: Free Press, n.d.), 81–203.

7. Gunnar Myrdal, *An American Dilemma* (New York: Harper and Row, 1944), 929.

8. Kuhn, *Scientific Revolutions*, 66–76.

9. Parsons, *The Social System*, 505–20.

10. Whitehead, *Process and Reality*, 18.

11. Ibid.

12. Ibid.

13. F. Bradford Wallack, *The Epochal Nature of Process in Whitehead's Process Metaphysics* (Albany: State University of New York, 1980), 45.

14. Whitehead, *Process and Reality*, 18.

15. Ibid.

16. "Society of actual occasions" is the phrase Whitehead uses to describe tangible things in the world that maintain identity. For example, the human body consists of a society of actual occasions. While the actual occasions the human body is composed of appear to endure change and maintain sameness, in reality these occasions are constantly making a transition from potentiality into actuality just as all other occasions do. In other words, actual occasions are not static and unchanging.

17. Whitehead, *Process and Reality*, 21.

18. Whitehead, *Religion in the Making*, 113.

19. Ibid.

20. Ibid.

21. Whitehead, *Process and Reality*, 22.

22. Kuhn, *Scientific Revolutions*, 41.

23. Quoted from Wallack, *Whitehead's Metaphysics*, 130; see Milic Capek, *The Philosophical Impact of Contemporary Physics* (Princeton, N.J.: D. Van Nostrand Co., 1961).

24. Whitehead, *Science and the Modern World* (New York: Macmillan Co., 1925), 28.

25. Ibid.

26. Quoted in Horace Kallen, *Culture and Democracy in the United States* (New York: Boni and Liveright, 1924), 131. John Dewey and Horace Kallen pioneered in the development of the methodology and content of cultural pluralism. For an informed discussion of John Dewey's ideas about cultural pluralism, see Seymour W. Itzkoff, *Cultural Pluralism and American Education* (Philadelphia: International Textbook Co., 1969); also, important discussions of Horace Kallen's ideas about cultural pluralism can be found in *Vision and Action: Essays in Honor of Horace M. Kallen*, ed. Sidney Ratner (New York: Kennikat Press, 1969).

27. Kallen, *Culture and Democracy*, 132.

28. Parsons, *The Social System*, 327–28.

29. Martin Luther King, Jr., "The Challenge to the Churches and Synagogues," in *Challenge to Religion*, ed. Matthew Ahmann (Chicago: Henry Regnery Co., 1963), 155.

30. Quoted from Kallen, *Culture and Democracy*, 132.

31. Kuhn, *Scientific Revolutions*, 111.

32. Ibid., 111–12.

33. George F. Thomas, *Religious Philosophies of the West* (New York: Charles Scribner's Sons, 1965), 30–37.

34. Quoted from the King James Version of the Bible.

35. William Cecil Dampier, *History of Science* (New York: The Macmillan Co., 1949), 97–145.

36. W. E. B. Du Bois, *The World and Africa* (New York: International Publishers, 1965), 44–80.

37. John Hope Franklin, *From Slavery to Freedom* (New York: Vintage Books, 1967), 42.

38. Du Bois, *The World and Africa*, 20.

39. Constance Baker Motley, "The Legal Status of the Negro in the United States," in *The American Negro Reference Book*, ed. John P. Davis (Englewood Cliffs, N.J.: Prentice Hall, n.d.), does a thorough analysis of the status of Afro-Americans from the time of slavery to the present.

40. See Whitehead, *Concept of Nature* (New York: Cambridge University Press, 1978), 1–48.

41. Martin Buber pioneered in attempting to rescue modern humanity from relating to the world through utility. See Buber's discussion in *I and Thou* (New York: Charles Scribner's Sons, 1970).

42. Franklin, *From Slavery to Freedom*, 43–48.

43. Ibid., 43.

44. Jürgen Moltmann, *Experiences of God* (Philadelphia: Fortress Press, 1980), 58.

45. Richard Hofstadter, *Social Darwinism* (New York: George Braziller, 1959), 13–30.

46. Thomas F. Gossett, *Race* (Dallas: Southern Methodist University Press, 1963), 144–75.

47. Hofstadter, *Social Darwinism*, 170–200.

48. Whitehead, *Process and Reality*, 128–29.

49. John H. Milsum, "The Hierarchical Basis for General Living Systems," in *Trends in General Systems Theory*, ed. George J. Klir (New York: Wiley-Interscience, 1971), 5.

50. *International Encyclopedia of the Social Sciences*, ed. David L. Sills (New York: Macmillan Co., 1968), 4:328–44.

51. Martin Luther King, Jr., *Where Do We Go from Here: Chaos or Community?* (Boston: Beacon Press, 1967), 167.

52. Shridath S. Ramphal, "Global Management Required for New Economic Order," *The North-South Dialogue* (March/April 1981): 6.

53. John Cobb, Jr., "Process Theology and Environmental Issues," *Journal of Religion* 60 (October 1980): 446.

54. Eugene P. Odum, *Fundamentals of Ecology* (Philadelphia: W. B. Saunders Co., 1971), 510–16.

55. Whitehead, *Concept of Nature*, 141.

56. Alfred North Whitehead, *Modes of Thought* (New York: The Macmillan Co., 1938), 152.

Chapter 3

1. John Macquarrie, *Principles of Christian Theology* (New York: Charles Scribner's Sons, 1977), 1–3.

2. George R. Stewart, *American Ways of Life* (New York: Doubleday and Co., 1954).

3. Will Herberg, *Protestant-Catholic-Jew: An Essay in American Religious Sociology* (New York: Doubleday and Co., 1955), 35.

4. For several excellent articles relating the empirical method to theology, see *The Future of Empirical Theology*, ed. Bernard Meland (Chicago: The University of Chicago Press, 1969).

5. John B. Cobb, Jr., *A Christian Natural Theology* (Philadelphia: Westminster Press, 1965), 28.

6. Alfred North Whitehead, *Process and Reality* (New York: The Free Press, 1978), 5-6.

7. Bernard Loomer, "Whitehead's Method of Empirical Analysis," in *Process Theology*, ed. Ewert H. Cousins (New York: Newman Press, 1971), 67-82.

8. Talcott Parsons, *The Social System* (New York: Free Press, 1964), 24-112, describes cultural patterns as commitment to certain values within a culture. After social groups in a culture integrate certain values with persistence to the extent that the values become integral to life-style, they develop into cultural patterns.

9. Whitehead, *Process and Reality*, 49.

10. Frederick Copleston, *A History of Philosophy*, vol. 1, pt. 1 (New York: Doubleday, 1962), 93-97.

11. See Ivor Leclerc's discussion of Whitehead's response to Plato's theory of forms in "Whitehead and the Theory of Form," in *Process and Divinity*, ed. William L. Reeves and Eugene Freeman (Chicago: Open Court Pub. Co., 1964), 127-37.

12. George F. Thomas, *Religious Philosophies of the West* (New York: Charles Scribner's Sons, 1965), 27-45.

13. Whitehead, *Process and Reality*, 79.

14. Ibid., 88.

15. F. Bradford Wallack, *The Epochal Nature of Process in Whitehead's Process Metaphysics* (Albany: State University of New York, 1980), 76.

16. Bernard Lonergan, *Method in Theology* (New York: Herder and Herder, 1972), 4.

17. Paul Tillich, *Systematic Theology* (Chicago: The University of Chicago Press, 1963), 1:40-46.

18. The nature of religious experience requires that it transcend what is verifiable.

19. Ludwig Feuerbach, for example, creates a phenomenological approach that fails to describe the self as a historical phenomenon conditioned by sociocultural factors. This can be seen in *The Essence of Christianity* (New York: Harper and Row, 1957).

20. The atomistic model in process metaphysics is organic. Each occasion of experience contains both internal and external interrelatedness.

21. Tillich, *Systematic Theology*, 1:3–8.

22. Martin Luther King, Jr., *Where Do We Go from Here: Chaos or Community?* (Boston: Beacon Press, 1967), 180.

23. Ibid., 181.

24. Tillich, *Systematic Theology*, 1:34–46.

25. Tillich, *History of Christian Theology* (New York: Simon and Schuster, 1968), 388–410.

26. Ibid.

27. Ibid.

28. Tillich, *The Courage To Be* (New Haven: Yale University Press, 1952), 182–90.

29. Whitehead, *Process and Reality*, 88.

30. Ibid.

31. Tillich, *Systematic Theology*, 1:163–241.

32. Ibid.

33. Ibid., 106–59.

34. Rudolf Bultmann, *Jesus Christ and Mythology* (New York: Charles Scribner's Sons, 1958), 11–21.

35. Ibid., 18.

36. Since its inception, not only has the black church served as the basis of African survivals, but it has always been the vanguard of social, economic, and political activism in the black community.

37. See Lawrence C. Jones, "They Sought a City: The Black Church and Churchmen in the Nineteenth Century," *Union Seminary Quarterly* 26/3 (Spring 1971): 253–72; and Robert T. Handy, "Negro Christianity and American Church Historiography," in *Essays in Divinity*, vol. 5, *Reinterpretation in American Church History*, ed. Jerald C. Brauer (Chicago: University of Chicago Press, 1968), 91–112.

38. Teilhard de Chardin, *The Phenomenon of Man* (New York: Harper and Row, 1959), 33.

39. Jones, "They Sought a City," 253–54.

40. Ibid.

41. See Gayraud S. Wilmore, *Black Religion and Black Radicalism* (Garden City, N.Y.: Anchor Press/Doubleday, 1973).

42. Strands of black separatism can be found in Garveyism, black nationalism, Pan-Africanism, and the early formation of the Black Muslim movement in America.

43. Jones, "They Sought a City," 253–72.

44. See Kenneth L. Smith and Ira G. Zepp, Jr., *Search for the Beloved Com-*

munity: The Thinking of Martin Luther King, Jr. (Valley Forge, Pa.: Judson Press, 1974).

45. Whitehead, *Function of Reason,* 5.

46. Daniel Day Williams, "Deity, Monarch and Metaphysics," in *The Relevance of Whitehead,* 360.

47. William M. Urban, "Whitehead's Philosophy of Language," in *The Philosophy of Whitehead,* ed. Paul Arthur Schilpp (Evanston, Il.: Northwestern University, 1941).

Chapter 4

1. Rem B. Edwards, *Reason and Religion* (New York: Harcourt Brace, 1972), 190.

2. Whitehead, *Process and Reality* (New York: The Free Press, 1978), 343.

3. Ibid., 29.

4. Christian, *Introduction to Whitehead's Metaphysics* (New Haven: Yale University Press, 1959), 364–81.

5. Whitehead, *Process and Reality,* 348.

6. Ibid., 239.

7. Ibid., 348–49.

8. I think that the dualistic perspective, consequently, is contrary to the authentic roots of Africans, Afro-Americans, and the Judeo-Christian heritage.

9. Joseph Klausner, *The Messianic Idea in Israel* (New York: The Macmillan Co., 1955), 10–11.

10. J. A. T. Robinson, *The Body* (London: SCM Press, 1952), 19.

11. John S. Pobee, *Toward an African Theology* (Nashville: Abingdon Press, 1979), 43–52.

12. Ibid.

13. Laurenti Magesa, "Authentic African Spirituality," in *African Christian Spirituality* (Maryknoll, N.Y.: Orbis Books, 1978), 74.

14. Ibid.

15. John S. Mbiti, *African Religions and Philosophies* (New York: Doubleday, 1970), 2.

16. Ibid., 6.

17. Martin Luther King, Jr., "Letter from Birmingham Jail," in *Justice Denied,* ed. William M. Chace and Peter Collier (New York: Harcourt Brace and World, 1970), 343.

18. Ibid.

19. Whitehead, *Adventures of Ideas* (New York: Macmillan, 1933), 217.

20. Ibid., 213.

21. Whitehead, *Science and the Modern World* (New York: Macmillan Co., 1925), 179.

22. Ibid., 190–91.

23. Tillich, *The Courage To Be* (New Haven: Yale University Press, 1952), 185.

24. Lewis S. Ford, "Divine Persuasion and the Triumph of Good," in *Process Philosophy and Christian Thought*, ed. Delwin Brown, Ralph E. James, Jr., and Gene Reeves (New York: Bobbs-Merrill Co., n.d.), 297.

25. Frederick Douglass, "No Progress without Struggle," in *The Black Power Revolt*, ed. Floyd B. Barbour (New York: Collier Books, 1968), 36–37.

26. Whitehead, *Adventures of Ideas*, 213.

27. Whitehead, *Process and Reality*, 346.

28. Ibid.

29. Whitehead, *Science and the Modern World*, 178.

30. Ibid.

31. See Christian, *Introduction to Whitehead's Metaphysics*, 388–90.

32. Charles Hartshorne, *Man's Vision of God and the Logic of Theism* (Chicago: Willett, Clark and Co., 1941), 195.

33. See David Griffin, *God, Power, and Evil: A Process Theodicy* (Philadelphia: Westminster Press, 1976).

34. Whitehead, *Process and Reality*, 342–51.

35. Ibid., 346.

36. Ibid., 340.

37. Ibid., 25.

38. Ibid., 351.

39. Ibid.

40. Ibid., 346.

41. Ibid., 346–47.

42. Ibid., 346.

43. Whitehead, *Religion in the Making* (New York: The Macmillan Co., 1926), 94.

44. Ibid., 98–99.

45. Ibid., 96.

46. Ibid., 95.

47. Whitehead, *Adventures of Ideas*, 369.

48. Jürgen Moltmann, "Response to the Opening Presentations," in *Hope and the Future of Man*, ed. Ewert H. Cousins (Philadelphia: Fortress, 1972), 57.

49. Martin Luther King, Jr., *Where Do We Go from Here: Chaos or Community?* (Boston: Beacon Press, 1967), 171.

Index